THE GIFT OF CONNECTION

THE GIFT OF CONNECTION

RECLAIMING THE POWER OF PRESENCE IN THE AGE OF DISTRACTION

MARK OSTACH

WILEY

Published by John Wiley & Sons, Inc., Hoboken, New Jersey.

Library of Congress Cataloging-in-Publication Data is Available:

ISBN 9781394381302 (Cloth)
ISBN 9781394381326 (ePDF)
ISBN 9781394381319 (ePUB)

Cover Design: Shawn McConnell
Cover Image: Tatiana/stock.adobe.com
Author Photo: Ksenija Savic Ostach

SKY10162806_071626

To our children's children

Contents

Foreword

I first met Mark over 20 years ago. I was serving as a judge at a business pitch competition, where a young entrepreneur took the stage with a bold idea and a clear sense of purpose. He was competing for a $10,000 prize, pitching a company he had founded based on something he called the *psychology of technology*, software designed to help people better manage their time and mood online.

He didn't win that day.

But what struck me then, and what has only become more evident with time, was that Mark wasn't just pitching a product. He was pointing to a future.

Over the past two decades, I've watched that early vision steadily catch up with the reality we now live in: a world where technology shapes our attention, influences our emotions, and quietly competes for our presence.

And today, that tension has only intensified.

We are living in a moment when artificial intelligence is accelerating how we work, decide, and communicate. We are more connected than ever before, and yet many people feel more distracted, depleted, and disconnected than ever. The pace is relentless. The noise is constant. And the cost of losing our presence is higher than we realize.

Because when we lose our presence, we don't just lose focus. We lose clarity in our decisions, depth in our relationships, and a sense of meaning in the moments that matter most.

What makes Mark's work so powerful is that he doesn't just diagnose the problem. He offers a way forward.

This book is not about rejecting technology or longing for a simpler time. It's about reclaiming something essential in the midst of it all. Through stories, insights, and practical reflection, Mark invites us to rediscover the power of presence, not as a luxury but as a leadership advantage and a deeply human necessity.

And the payoff is real. When you learn to be fully present, you lead with greater clarity, connect with greater authenticity, and experience your work and life with a renewed sense of energy and purpose.

I've had the privilege of watching Mark live this message. Whether on stage, in conversation, or in the quiet moments in between, he has a rare ability to meet people where they are and remind them of what matters most.

That's what you'll find in these pages.

This is a book that will challenge you to slow down, to pay attention, and to reconnect with yourself, with others, and with the life you're building.

So don't rush through it.

Read it with intention. Reflect as you go. And allow it to recalibrate not just how you work but also how you live.

Because in a world that rewards speed, the real advantage belongs to those who can be fully present.

—Josh Linkner, *New York Times* bestselling author,
tech entrepreneur, jazz guitarist

Introduction

I am a man of two very different worlds.

Born in the early 1980s, I became a teenager smack dab in the middle of what many (at least according to Instagram) call the greatest decade in modern American history: the 1990s.

Baggy jeans. Ping pong in the basement with friends. Hot Pockets and Cool Ranch Doritos fueling endless rounds of *John Madden Football* and *Sonic the Hedgehog*. We were masters of the mixtape and experts at doing absolutely nothing for hours—without once feeling bored.

Back then, connection meant calling your best friend on a corded phone to see if they could "play." If you liked someone, you passed a folded note in pre-algebra with three boxes to check: yes, no, or maybe. And if they took all day to respond, you waited—because that's just how life worked.

The laughter. The waiting. The simplicity of it all.

We didn't have screens in our pockets or cameras recording every moment. Our focus was on the moment, our hands were free, and our attention was in the room.

Then there was my pager, pure coolness in rectangular form. Thanks to my mom's job at the phone company, I even had a customized number: 400-MARK. We used secret number codes to send upside-down messages, most of them too juvenile to repeat here.

My mom had the original pager, the dinner bell on our front porch. Back then, we spent endless afternoons playing sports, riding bikes, and getting into mostly innocent mischief. Our eyes were rarely pointed downward. We were always looking up toward the next adventure. It wasn't perfect, but it felt like we were living actual life.

By high school, I graduated to my first flip phone. Suddenly, I felt cooler than Zack Morris from *Saved by the Bell*, minus the blond hair and the ability to pause time. The rules were simple: you either got a call or you didn't. You couldn't track anyone or tell if they were online and ignoring you. You just waited.

The only thing I loved more than that phone was my Walkman cassette deck. If you wanted to hear past song six, you flipped the tape from Side A to Side B. If you wanted to replay a track, you held rewind and waited. Instead of scrolling, you looked around, made eye contact, and tried to look cool leaning against the wall in your oversized New Kids on the Block T-shirt, just hangin' tough.

I guess you could say my life is like one of those old cassette tapes: it has two sides.

The exact year of my birth, 1981, is considered by some to be the last year of Generation X, while others call it the first year of the millennials. Like someone straddling a state line, I have a foot in two places at once. Those of us born in these few years are sometimes called *Xennials* or the *Oregon Trail Generation*, a nod to the dazzling 4-bit graphics of the early Apple II game where getting dysentery was somehow still fun.

My life has two halves: pre-digital and post-internet. I hold a rare vantage point, one of the few people left on the planet with an analog childhood and a digital adulthood.

I've used rotary pay phones and iPhones. I've written papers with the lost art of cursive and I've written emails using artificial intelligence (AI). I've manually balanced a checkbook and downloaded budgeting apps. The thing is, both sides of my life's cassette tape are good.

This is not an anti-technology manifesto. There are no torches, pitchforks, or the storming of any digital castles (not even sure how that would work). Technology is revolutionizing medicine, connecting global cultures, and providing pathways of education to millions who never had one before. Odds are, this book either physically came to you through the use of technology (like Amazon or Barnes and Noble) or is literally being read on a digital device. You should not feel guilty before, after, or during this reading because I am not against technology.

I am for humanity—your humanity.

If you're like me, you could use all the human friends you can get right now. You probably sense it too, how easy it is to feel increasingly alone and isolated, even as we connect with more people online than ever before. We live in a unique moment in human history where AI reshapes communication daily. Our brains are constantly stimulated by screens, notifications, and endless scrolls.

Research suggests that within a few years (and likely by the time this book is published), more than 90% of online content will be generated by bots.[1] Various influencers and researchers hypothesize nearly 40% of AI prompts relate to mental health or loneliness. Modern humanity is turning to technology for comfort and connection rather than to each other—and for all its benefits, this part isn't working. The world is beginning to wake up to this truth. A growing number of initiatives, including a brilliant marketing campaign called "Go Offline" launched by Pinterest this April, demonstrate the call for more real-world experiences. People are becoming exhausted from maintaining their lives both online and offline.

In one of my TED Talks, I described how we live with *i-Drenaline*—a digital form of adrenaline. Every buzz, notification, or scroll triggers a microburst of dopamine. We feel phantom vibrations even when our phones aren't there. Our minds and bodies now crave something that didn't exist at the beginning of the new millennium.

Like a time traveler between two eras, I'm writing to remind you of the power of connection—connection with people who have real, beating hearts. Because no matter what advances technology brings, the human heart remains the greatest technology ever created. It will always surpass anything built by human hands.

But before I could remind anyone else of these truths, my wife had to remind me.

Losing and Finding My Why

To be honest, writing this book has been much harder than I anticipated. I've written several other books, but this one feels different. It has required a different level of authenticity and accessing it has been hard, but worth it in the end. Candidly, this is also the first time in my journey of writing books when ChatGPT has been an available tool. I hear that many writers are struggling to keep their craft honest and also be wise in using modern technology. Sometimes, what I want to write is not what Chat wants me to write. Just so you know, in the end I scrapped everything Chat wanted to write and reached out instead to a human friend with whom I could collaborate and flesh out the inner tensions of my heart.

At one point, I nearly quit altogether. I was exhausted and stuck in a familiar spiral of self-doubt and shame. I had written and rewritten so many of these words so many times and I was just mentally exhausted. I had finally come to an impasse with myself. Thankfully my wife, Ksenija (pronounced Sen-ya), helped me get unstuck.

Not only is she my best friend and mother of our two children and three dogs, she also has been my copyeditor over the past 15 years. She has often gently reminded me of the man I want to become, and helped me find the next step to becoming that person. Without her, you would not be reading these words.

It was nearly midnight and Ksenija could see I was spiraling. She said in a soft voice, "You've lost your why for this book, haven't you?"

I sighed in shame. "Yeah, I think so."

She continued, "Do you know where it went?"

I just shrugged.

A long pause ensued. "I think I know where it is," she said. I looked up as we locked eyes. "Your why is sleeping in those rooms right down that hall." Tears filled my eyes. "Mark, write this book for our children—and for their children."

It was just what I needed to hear!

This conversation reignited my focus and drive to finish writing this book.

What You Can Expect

This book is both a wake-up call and an invitation. In the pages ahead, you'll explore how the rise of distraction and digital overload is quietly shaping the way we think, work, lead, and relate to one another.

Through personal stories, research, and reflection questions, you'll discover how to reclaim your attention, strengthen your relationships, and hopefully be more present in your everyday life.

At the end of the book, I'll leave you with the GIFTS Framework—Grace, Intentionality, Focus, Trust, and Sensitivity—a practical model designed to help you foster deeper awareness and more meaningful connection in a world constantly competing for your attention.

Before we officially dive in though, I do want to make one disclaimer.

One Quick Disclaimer

I'll admit it. I've always been good at connecting with people.

When I was seven years old, I invited our priest over for dinner while he was shaking hands after Mass. My mom was mortified. She hadn't prepared for guests and silently prayed he'd say no. To my disappointment and her relief, he declined the impulsive invitation.

Thirty years later, while traveling as a speaker, I made a fancy dinner reservation for one, hoping to catch my breath after a long day. Then I stepped onto an elevator and within 15 seconds struck up a conversation with a group of well-dressed strangers on their way to a large church conference. I skipped my dinner and ended up as the only white guy in a room of 400 Black churchgoers dressed to the nines, opening a three-day event with a three-hour service. They escorted me to the front row like I was a VIP. Let's just say I never ate dinner that night.

Then there was the time I struck up a conversation with a homeless man on the streets of Detroit. What began as a passing exchange turned into a four-hour walk. It's a story I'm still trying to understand.

Please don't misunderstand me. This book isn't about talking to strangers in elevators or on the streets. And it's certainly not about being "naturally good" at connection.

My hope is simpler and bigger.

I want to help you rethink your own ability to see, speak, and spark meaningful connection with the people around you. As you read these stories, I ask you to resist the thought: *Wow, Mark is just a natural. I could never do that.*

You're halfway right. You'll never be like me. And that's the best news you'll hear all day.

You don't need to be like me.

You need to be like you.

Yes, we'll explore research, insights, and practical ways to foster connection. But those aren't the point. They aren't the gift.

You are.

Connection isn't reserved for special occasions. It waits for us in everyday moments, in break rooms, classrooms, jobsites, and call centers. The most gifted connectors I've met aren't CEOs or nonprofit leaders. They're ordinary people living ordinary lives, quietly creating extraordinary moments.

The common denominator of great connectors is simple.

They share more of themselves.

They are great listeners.

They believe the greatest technology isn't *out there*. It's within.

My bet is you're the same.

You don't need to become someone new.

You simply need to remember who you already are and find your way back to the gift you already carry.

THE GIFT OF CONNECTION

PART I

The Inner Gift: Awakening to Presence

Before we can connect outward, we must awaken inward.

1 Digital Pulse

"We become what we pay attention to."

—**William James**

To live, your heart—the greatest technology on earth—has to keep beating in rhythm. Your heart beats 100,000 times per day, 36 million times per year, and nearly 2.9 billion times in an average lifetime (if you live to be 80 years old). That's a lot of heartbeats.

But the modern heartbeat is different than any other time in history. Research shows that the average 18-year-old today will spend roughly 21 of their 80 years on a screen![1] That suggests that one quarter of your life, or nearly 800 million of your heartbeats, will reverberate in the digital world.

Thankfully, your pulse reflecting these heartbeats reminds you that you're alive. This physical pulse has a baseline rhythm that is steady and predictable, regardless of your heart rate increasing or decreasing. If your heart gets out of rhythm, it is a sign of something unhealthy like an arrhythmia or A-fib. But I'd like to introduce you to another term specific to our modern life: *digital pulse*. Your digital pulse functions opposite of your physical one. Its baseline is a chaotic rhythm. It starts in A-fib, or better said, D-fib. This is because of the nature of digital content and platforms. They are all over the place on purpose.

On any normal morning, your brain processes a news story about war in Eastern Europe followed by a cute meme of a baby hugging a puppy. Maybe you post a pic of your kindergartner before school—and you're so proud (as you should be). Next, you repost an inspirational quote from your favorite author (aw, you shouldn't have!). It's not that anything you've done is necessarily bad; it's just all over the place. It has no consistent rhythm. The digital pulse isn't set into rhythm for the purpose of keeping you breathing. It is shocked into divergent reactive rhythms for the purpose of making you catch your breath.

By the time the afternoon hits, you're keeping up on your stories and you're seeing your inbox continue to fill up with messages you haven't responded to. The red numbered circle of notifications on three of your social media thumbnails show more than 50 unread things demanding your action before they can be cleared. Your digital pulse begins to move back and forth from frantic to faint. It reveals the pressure you feel not only to be on all the time but also that if you don't respond to someone or something, you're dead to the world. Your digital pulse feels like the only way to prove to the world that you're still alive and a part of the collective culture and conversation. Without your online presence, would anyone out there even know you're here?

Have you ever had someone say to you, "Hey, are you doing okay?" I sent you a text a couple days ago and I hadn't heard back from you. I was wondering if something went wrong?" This probably made you slightly angry or even guilty of the fact you can't keep up with all of your digital chores of responding to every message that crossed your digital day. And if you feel the pressure with your friends, imagine the pressure you feel at the workplace.

In fact, I've heard from some remote employees about something called *the spoon trick*. A person using this hack places a spoon on their computer mouse to keep their Microsoft Teams status green, giving the illusion that they are active while actually they are doing laundry, working out, or taking a power nap. This reveals how even the workplace has become a place of constant digital demand. We simply can't be everywhere at once, so we are forced to fake being present just to survive. Have you been there? I know I have.

It's hard enough to sustain the day-to-day demands of one's physical life, but to sustain two lives within the same body is impossible. Our digital pulse makes us fall victim to an internalized digital obligation to be constantly present and responsive. Our brains crave the quick dopamine hits that seem to make us "feel alive," but they actually dysregulate our inner rhythms into perpetual, unpredictable chaos.

Humans, you see, are not made to maintain or regulate two pulses. One will eventually disrupt the other. The ancient Chinese philosopher Lao Tzu is purported to have said, "Those who flow as life flows know they need no other force." But the truth is, most of us are not flowing, we are buffering. We start to move, then pause, scroll, and stall. That constant start-and-stop rhythm is what I call *life lagging*.

Life Lagging

Life lagging is the gap between how long something should take and how long it actually takes because of distraction. See if you can connect with this example:

HONK!

We have all heard it, the honk at the green light when your head is still down. You look up, embarrassed, and wave an apologetic "sorry" to the car behind you. Multiply that tiny delay by millions of moments each day, and you start to see it: life lagging in action. Each quick glance at a phone, each "just a sec" notification, each tiny pause adds up to time lost and patience drained.

Apps like Google Maps and Waze know this better than anyone. When you see those red lines of traffic ahead, they are not guessing. They are tracking the collective lag of thousands of drivers. One distracted moment here, another there, and soon an entire highway slows to a crawl. The same thing happens in life. Our attention gets jammed. We think we are moving, but we are actually idling in a digital traffic jam of our own making.

Rinse and repeat. We inch forward, having lost those three seconds of time. But across all of society, each of those three-second delays adds up to huge amounts of time lost, energy wasted, and anger or embarrassment felt by the honk givers and the honk receivers. Every day, thousands of hours are affecting millions of people making it to their destinations on time—or even at all. The technology that is meant to help us get ahead faster is actually causing us to lag behind. It is death by a thousand paper cuts of delay. It is not just a traffic issue; it is a life issue.

We are life lagging.

And it is not just on the road; it is everywhere. Take Costco, for example. You notice the perfect parking spot. The car's brake lights glow red. You wait for it to back out. And wait. And wait. But the car does not move. The driver is sitting there, idling, ensuring their digital pulse is alive and well. Scrolling. Liking. Replying. All the while, you are stuck in a holding pattern, watching your chance at free samples slip away. Their lagging is literally keeping you from replenishing your stash of paper towels and toilet paper!

The same thing happens in our homes. In our family, my wife usually makes the kids' lunches because she is a creative genius in the kitchen. When she makes them, the kids experience all the tastes and colors of the culinary rainbow. In the case of these school lunches, variety truly is the spice of life. When I make the lunches, not so much. But I make them substantially faster than she does. The variety may be missing, but the task gets accomplished in a fraction of the time. (Guess which lunches the kids prefer.)

In this lunch-making family odyssey, I have noticed a trend: the whole process often leaves my wife frustrated. I will see her take out the peanut butter and jelly to start the task while I take the kids upstairs to make sure they are not fighting over who is using mom and dad's bathroom. I get them finished with a 30-minute shower and lead them through the nightly process of brushing their teeth without sword fighting—or stabbing—each other with their toothbrushes. (Again, it is an odyssey.) But when I come back downstairs, I often find the containers still open and the dry bread slices still begging for a little peanut butter and jelly.

The thing is, my wife is still standing there. Her phone, however, is held up to her mouth on speaker as she finishes sending a three-minute audio message to a friend whom I did not even know she had been talking to. Somewhere between spreading the peanut butter and sealing the sandwich bag, a message popped up on her phone. Then another. Someone needed a recipe. Someone else needed prayer. A friend shared a struggle. She listened, cared, and responded because that is who she is, an encourager. But the lunches are still sitting half-made, the peanut-butter jar open, the knife midair. It is not her fault. It is life lagging again.

Even when our hearts are in the right place, our attention is divided. Take sleep, for example: how many mornings do you wake feeling tired wishing you would have gotten more rest? Now think about how your phone affects your nighttime routine. Just consider that, rather than sleeping, when we add an extra 30 minutes each night on the phone over the course of 30 days, the lag adds up to a loss of 15 hours of sleep (30 minutes × 30 days = 900 minutes/60 = 15 hours).

Divided attention always costs us something: time, peace, patience, or rest. That is life lagging, the collision of good intentions and divided attention. It is not malicious. It is just modern. But it is slowly robbing us of something far more valuable than time: our sense of rhythm, flow, and presence in the world around us.

The Age of Distraction

Our digital pulse is accelerating, while our human lives are lagging, creating what I call the *Age of Distraction*. Ours is a moment in history defined not by a lack of information, but by an overwhelming excess of it. Heck, I was a paperboy for two years in the early 1990s and the only "news" I consumed was the first five minutes of the local 6 p.m. news right after an episode of *The Simpsons*. Nowadays, our devices are faster than ever, our feeds never stop, and our attention is pulled in countless directions at once. To understand how we arrived here and why hope still matters, it helps to step back and look at the eras that have shaped the world before us—and that could shape the world ahead of us, if we dare to hope and dream.

Era	**Approximate Time Frame**	**Defining Influence**
Industrial Age	1900–1940s	Machines, productivity, efficiency
Atomic Age	1945–1960s	Power, progress, existential risk
Television Age	1950s–1980s	Mass media, shared narratives
Information Age	1990s–2000s	Computers, internet, access
Social Media Age	2000–2010s	Connectivity, visibility, validation
Age of Distraction	2015–Present	Speed, overload, fractured attention
Age of Presence?	Future	Intention, connection, wisdom

As the world continues to spin, my hope is that this book ignites within us a shared intention for our world to be more present and focused on true connection through wisdom, wonder, and the greatest gift of all: you!

You Are a Gift

This is a book for humans. (No offense to any bots out there—you are also welcome to buy a copy. Or to put it into words you can understand "01001000 01101001" ["Hi"].) But this book is about navigating the rising tensions of balancing our shared humanity with our ever-widening digitality. If you're like me, when you lose this balance, you lose something much more critical: the gift of yourself.

Human connection remains our greatest need because each of us is a gift created for continual exchange and mutual connection to others, who are also gifts in their own right. But *connection* has become such a buzzword that we struggle to muster a practical understanding or approach to finding it. We crave it and resist it at the same time.

The chaotic pulse is in conflict with the steady pulse. And we often don't even know why this tension exists.

This is why the unique challenges of the Age of Distraction require us to adopt a more intentional approach to human connection, one that begins by awakening both to what fosters presence in our lives and what robs us of it. As we have become more individualized and less connected, it is easy to feel and believe that what consumes our thinking and habits is harmless. Who cares if I spend four hours scrolling on my phone? It's not like I'm hurting anybody?

But if your pulse is dysregulated, it affects both you and everyone around you—just ask someone giving first aid or CPR. That's why we need to look into how your online habits shape how you see yourself, how you see others, and how you see our future together. Again, this doesn't mean we need to stop using technology. We just need to stop being ignorant to how it affects us, whether positively and negatively.

Back in the 1990s, when you wanted to wash your car, you would buy one of these huge yellow sponges—the kind that could soak up a bathtub of water. Your brain, your mind, and your heart are like one big sponge. Every morning, what you dip that sponge into is what's going to ring out of it for the rest of the day. You already know this from your own honest experience, but the data also supports the fact most of us reach for our phones in the morning before we've even used the bathroom or brushed our teeth.

To borrow from another metaphor, it's like waking up and immediately taking in huge helpings of sugary, dense, digital calories through news headlines, notifications, and reels. Within minutes, these empty digital calories leave you feeling bloated, overstimulated, and fearful of the future all at the same time—and all before you've even gotten out of bed!

If you consider yourself an average user on Facebook, you probably check your profile once an hour, often just to fill the space of a quiet or boring moment. Scrolling through dozens of posts and skimming the birthdays, baby announcements, and beautiful pictures of loved ones disrupts your fear of stillness. Of course, not everything you're digesting during this scroll session is uplifting. Much is just the opposite: death notices, car accidents, natural disasters, and other reasons to worry.

Although these are real parts of life, traumatic news has become the new norm for information. Here's a few more headlines during a recent scroll in the park:

- Breaking: School lockdown after threat posted online
- War escalates overnight as global leaders warn of wider conflict
- New virus variant detected as health officials urge caution
- Teen hospitalized after viral social media challenge
- Mass shooting dominates feeds as details emerge in real time
- Wildfires force evacuations as climate extremes intensify
- AI-generated deepfake sparks outrage and confusion
- Influencer death trends across platforms within minutes
- Missing child alert floods phones nationwide

Although these topics warrant being shared, sheer volume of our exposure to disaster and fear is dangerous to our emotional and spiritual health. But we do it anyway, mainly because our brains like to be aroused. The amygdala (our emotional center) becomes activated when we process traumatic news during an innocent scroll. Better known for the fight-or-flight response, the amygdala releases a chemical cascade of adrenaline and cortisol, a stress hormone intended to help us run from a dangerous situation. Now, we feel it all the time.

Post-Traumatic Scroll Disorder

The amygdala struggles to decipher between trauma in our virtual world and trauma in our physical world. Nowadays, such traumatic posts fuel our dates and dinner table conversations, planning seeds of fear in our fertile minds. It's no wonder our bodies are constantly tired from being dragged along by the undertows of the tidal wave of trauma we call normal scrolling. If you find yourself being force-fed emotionally charged posts on Facebook or TikTok, beware because your foundation is susceptible to heartache and stress. Hairline fractures in our personal psyches come from spikes in adrenaline and from exhaustion leading to what I call *post-traumatic scroll disorder.*

Post-traumatic *stress* disorder is a serious mental health condition that has afflicted some of my friends and family. But I've literally seen loved ones mentally suffer from what they've seen on social media. Even if they don't click on the post to read more, the fact that they've exposed their minds to even the headline of such news can hinder their perspective for the entire day, week, or longer. Innocent scrolling yields feelings of sadness, depression, and dread. Can you agree that maybe we're being traumatized more than we realize?

For example, I was with my wife purchasing a new used car. It was a significant moment as we had been saving up for a few years and waiting for the right car to buy. After months of research, and way too many searches on Facebook Marketplace, the day had arrived. We scheduled a day date to go pick up the new, certified used car, and even drove 90 minutes to the dealership. While we were waiting for paperwork to sign the deal, I turned to her and noticed she was looking rather sad. I paused and asked her what was the matter? She said with tears in her eyes, "James Van Der Beek just died."

I said, "The guy from *Dawson's Creek*?" To which she responded yes, as a few tears ran down her face.

Although this news is super sad and devastating to his family, it was colliding with a moment of excitement and joy moments before signing on the dotted line. Don't get me wrong, I'm not trying to sound insensitive, I'm just sharing how our digital lives can shape the mood of our real-life moments. Even though we didn't truly know James, he was a dad, husband, and about our age, so the real-time knowledge of his passing, created instant sadness and arousal within her brain. This example, is one of many that showcases a deep black hole of empathy for all of the sadness being shared on the internet to be dumped on the fertile soil of our hearts and brains.

All of this is a result of what I like to call *The Imitation Principle.* Simply put, your inputs become your output. If you are what you eat, then what you are consuming online on a daily basis (and how you consume it) is not harmless. No, it is literally shaping who you are and how you see the world. From serious geopolitical issues to funny viral memes that your kids spread like wildfire, we're all reflecting what we receive, for better or for worse. Everything you do—or don't do—shapes your heart in some way.

The good news is the modern technology swirling around you can't compete with the greatest technology beating within you. The trick is keeping the former from robbing the latter—not to lose the freedom and connection that make you the gift you are created to be. That's why I'm writing this book for you now: to share this little time capsule I'm leaving for my grandchildren as they navigate whatever confusion or opportunities arise between this moment and 80 years from now.

Yes, as you will hear in my own personal stories to come, sharing your heart can be messy, mucky, and painful. But you can develop the courage to disabuse your heart of the false narratives of isolation and disconnection being passed off as normal in the modern world. You can better know and better give to others the gift of yourself.

Reflection

When do you tend to fall into patterns of life lagging or find your digital pulse beating too fast?

2 The New Smoking

"What we habitually do becomes who we are."

—**Aristotle** *(paraphrased)*

I grew up in a blue-collar home in a suburb about 20 miles northwest of Detroit. Dad worked in the construction industry, and when I was young, my mother was a stay-at-home mom. My parents had four kids total: three boys and one girl. I shared a bedroom with my older brother, and I always slept on the bottom bunk. That is, until my younger brother came along. He was born with special needs and was better off with a sibling roommate, so my older brother moved to the basement and I moved to the top bunk to make way for my younger brother on the bottom bunk.

Little brothers usually look up to older brothers, even if they pick on them. It's just the way of the knucklehead—that is, the patterns of adolescent boys. One Christmas, my older brother and I each got a bike and boxing gloves. Let's just say that I enjoyed the bikes more than the boxing gloves. A funny VHS video still exists of us boxing one another in our matching Christmas pajamas. My brother was 14 years old and I was 12. All it took was one punch to land me on the floor. Dad was laughing, proud of his little men doing manly things, while Mom picked me up to put a tiny bag of cold ice on my eye. You know, Christmas.

One thing was for sure: I was ready to grow up so I could be strong enough to go toe-to-toe with my brother. I craved more control over my life, which is natural. By seventh grade, I was entering the testosterone-laden stage of early puberty. It wasn't pretty, but at least I was finally able to stand up to my brother. Still, I wasn't as strong as him, which probably explained why I got cut from the middle school basketball team. Well, and the little matter of not being able to make a left-handed layup. It was a bummer; however, I was beginning to come into my own.

As if on cue, I also developed my first crush: Lindsay Misch. She had beautiful blond hair that stretched for miles. Imagine my exhilaration when the art teacher sat us next to each other in class, close enough to smell Lindsay's perfume. Things were definitely trending in the right direction.

Since I didn't have basketball practice, I had extra time in the afternoons to hang out with my friends. One day in particular, my buddy came over and we decided to ride bikes to the school. The only problem was that my friend didn't have his bike, so I gave him mine and I borrowed my brother's. When we got to the school and went to lock up the bikes, I opened the little pouch on my brother's bike where he usually kept his lock. But instead, I found a pack of cigarettes.

See previous mentions of curiosity and testosterone in order to decipher what happened next. Yep, we decided to smoke the cigarettes. A wooded area was next to the school parking lot, so we snuck off into the woods while no one was looking. After all, if a middle school boy smokes a cigarette near a tree in the forest and no one's there to catch him, does he still make a hacking sound?

Yes. Yes, he does.

Truthfully, I think I barely inhaled, but the deed was done. I began to get nervous, hoping against hope that watermelon Bubblicious chewing gum would neutralize the smell of cigarette smoke. I remember sniffing my fingers to make sure they didn't reek of nicotine. I went home full of guilt and smelling like a sweaty chimney.

But we got away with it. After all, we were smooth operators. So what should you do if you barely get away with something that could land you in serious trouble? Do it again, of course! For the next two weeks, we kept smoking cigarettes in the woods. We were big men doing manly things.

Things also continued to go well with Lindsay. We danced together to "End of the Road" by Boyz II Men at a school dance. My hands were on her shoulders and her hands were on mine. We were swaying so far apart that my mom could have driven her 1985 station wagon between us with room to spare.

A few days later, Lindsay and I went to watch a school basketball game together. It was a big deal to sit by her in front of everyone—everything was coming up roses in my middle school world. The plan was that my mom would pick me up after the game—I only needed to call her on the school pay phone if it ended early or went into overtime.

Then it happened. Remember my mom's 1985 land yacht? It suddenly sailed into the school parking lot unannounced. The game was only in the first quarter. Suddenly, the side door near the basketball court flung wide open to reveal my mother marching into the gymnasium. She was a shorter woman, but I've never seen someone look more intimidating than she did in that moment. The whole gym froze as if Napoleon had just kicked down the door with his sword drawn. (Mom loves it when I compare her to Napoleon, BTW.) I don't remember her feet even touching the bleachers, as if she floated up the steps on tiny clouds of rage. She came right up to me and Lindsay and proceeded to take hold of my left ear.

"Let's go."

I was humiliated, but I dared not say anything. If you've never been led by the ear, you should try it sometime. Besides the surprisingly excruciating pain, it's not so bad. The walk of shame led us to the station wagon that was still idling and had probably wasted five gallons of gas in the three minutes my mom had been away. I've never seen her so angry, but she didn't say a word. Instead, she simply handed me a letter. I opened it, and what I read explained everything.

> Dear Mrs. Ostach, I've seen your son, Mark, smoking in the woods on multiple occasions the past few weeks. I'm a concerned parent and I figured you would want to know. Sincerely, Anonymous.

What We're Inhaling

Turns out, my seventh-grade compatriot and I weren't nearly as smooth as we thought. Not only was I grounded but I also assured my mom I would never smoke again. But why was my mom so upset? Because by the 1990s, the general public had finally accepted the fact that cigarettes are determinantal to one's health.

But it wasn't always this way. When American soldiers came home from World War I in 1918, they brought back with them an acquired taste for nicotine that they developed during their time in the trenches of Europe and the islands of the Pacific. Up to that point, cigarettes had been a novelty, but now they became mainstream. Aggressive marketing campaigns began promoting them as modern and sophisticated, so much so that by the 1940s and 1950s, they were seen as stylish, glamorous, and the social norm. Movies, advertising, and popular figures all normalized smoking. Heck, even Sheriff Andy Taylor smoked on *The Andy Griffith Show*.

Doctors smoked in delivery rooms. Airline passengers smoked in the confined pressurized cabins of airplanes. You could even smoke in restaurants. My point is that for almost half a century, hardly anyone questioned cigarettes. That's what happens when something is normalized, no matter how bad it might be for you.

How things have changed! I theorize that the current generation under 18 years of age will make smoking extinct in their lifetime. How did society move so very far in the opposite direction? Eventually, people finally began listening to the experts who were screaming from the rooftops about the health detriments of smoking. However, the most convincing variable was widespread lung cancer that eventually touched almost every family in America. It took a wave of disease and death to wake us up to the realities of their very real origins, which had been an accepted part of their daily routine for decades.

History doesn't necessarily repeat, but it often rhymes. We are prone to swap one vice for another. Clever experts now say that scrolling through social media is the new smoking for our generation.[1] I think they're right. It may sound dramatic, but the data and shared experiences of most Americans bear this out. We face an epidemic of real addiction. But unlike the advent of smoking that took many years to move from a fringe habit to your granny smoking in the kitchen, our addiction to scrolling has taken hold exponentially faster, all in the last decade or so.

In *The Anxious Generation*,[2] Jonathan Haidt presents a remarkable amount of research supporting how our digital lives are adversely affecting our mental health. And it's not just the younger generation who is anxious. It's all of us—we're all smoking. Anyone with a smartphone has purchased a pack of our modern version of cigarettes. We're not villains; we're just addicts. Our grandparents' generations of smokers never intended to make themselves sick or unhealthy. They just went along with the cultural norms of their day. After all, even their doctors were smoking, so how bad could it really be?

We must be committed to pushing past our phones and pursuing real connections because the personal and societal stakes have become so high. New research indicates that social connection and social well-being comprise the new mental health. In other words, mental health is no longer just about "random" diagnoses, though they still certainly exist. However, much of our mental health crisis is directly related to our issues with social connectivity.

In May 2023, the United States Surgeon General issued a formal advisory declaring loneliness and social isolation a public health epidemic in the United States. They found that nearly half of adults had reported experiencing loneliness. Furthermore, lacking social connection increases the risk for premature death to levels comparable to smoking 15 cigarettes a day. I don't mean that it's like 15 "mental" cigarettes. No, I mean that a lack of social connection is literally that drastically caustic to our overall physical health. This includes endless hours of doom scrolling, gaming, or even working behind a screen to the point that you're always plugged in and never at rest. As they say, the body keeps score, which is why poor social relationships increase the risk of heart disease by 29% and stroke by 32%. And among older adults, chronic loneliness increases the risk of developing dementia by approximately 50%. The advisory called for treating social connection with the same urgency as tobacco use, obesity, and addiction.[3]

In June 2025, a three-year commission created by the World Health Organization released its report: *From Loneliness to Social*

Connection: Charting a Path to Healthier Societies. They found that one in six people globally (15.8%) reported feeling lonely, while loneliness is linked to an estimated 100 deaths every hour. That's more than 871,000 deaths annually. People who are lonely are twice as likely to become depressed, and teenagers who feel lonely are 22% more likely to get lower grades. The report called on policymakers "to treat social health with the same urgency as physical and mental health."[4] About the same time, the World Health Assembly adopted the first-ever resolution on social connection, urging member states to develop evidence-based policies to promote social connection for mental and physical health.[5]

These are serious statistics, and we know they are exacerbated by our digital norms dictating our connection patterns. But we can be a part of the solution not just by studying these trends but also by effecting them through increased intentionality in our connection with others. No one should be seen online but invisible in real life. And yet, the data says this absolutely is the alarming trend we're experiencing at home and around the world.

Our current generations' new addiction is worse than smoking ever was because digital distraction separates us from the realities of connection with one another. Smoking could be a communal act, lighting up together after dinner or on a plane. But even though digital distraction happens alongside other people in our online worlds—and even though we interact with them in the process—we rarely feel a complete sense of community. This is why any online relationship that lasts generally does so because the online connection eventually leads people to gather in person at some point. Social media can be a gateway to human connection, but it cannot sustain human connection by itself.

That's why in December 2025, Australia became the first country to formally ban underage users (under the age of 16) from major social media platforms. The controversial step requires all major social media platforms to take "reasonable steps" to prevent underage access, using age-verification methods such as inference from online activity, facial estimation via selfies, uploaded IDs, or linked bank details.[6]

Most recently, in March 2026, Meta and Google were found liable for over $6 million in damages in a California social media addiction trial, marking a major legal defeat regarding addictive design and child safety. Additionally, a New Mexico court ordered Meta to pay $375 million for misleading users about platform safety for children. Although Meta intends to appeal these rulings, you can begin to see the heightened awareness of both the public eye and the policies shaping the future of our life online.[7]

At the time of this writing, the world is watching, aware of the issues our online habits create, but still trying to figure the appropriate response.

The pandemic made us more aware that social well-being is critical to our overall mental health. We learned how we must fight the pace and expectations of the modern age that rob us of our freedom. Because our lives are so digitally full, we have to be more intentional than ever to pursue community and unity. In the 1980s and 1990s, there was more room for spontaneity in the form of neighborhood gatherings and block parties. We would close down the block, order some pizzas, the adults would have some adult beverages, and the kids would spend the next six hours playing four-square and trying to get the straws successfully inserted in our Capri Suns.

The modern life leaves little room for spontaneity, but that doesn't mean we can't find the same level of connection, community, and belonging that past generations had. We just have to be more intentional to seek it. After all, as long as we're all still human, there's always potential for human connection. And no human is exempt from this deepest felt need.

Reflection

Which digital habits have become so normalized in your life that you rarely question their impact on your health, relationships, or sense of aliveness?

3

The Illusion of "Fine"

"Be kind, for everyone you meet is fighting a hard battle."

—**Ian Maclaren**

You never know where people are in life, which is why it's important to pursue connection with intentionality and as a way of living. The next part of my own story will bear out these truths in both beautiful and painful ways.

After high school, I went to Albion College, a small liberal arts school about 90 miles west of my hometown. I pursued a degree in psychology and neuroscience. My parents had three kids in college at once, so by the time I graduated, I had accrued $100,000 of student loan debt, which meant it was time to go to work!

When asked what I was going to do after college, I looked my dad squarely in the eyes and uttered the words every father wants to hear: "I think I'm gonna go to massage therapy school." It may have seemed like an odd choice for a guy with a new degree, but I had become super interested in workplace wellness. I also felt that I had a special gift of being able to use my hands to help people who were hurting.

Massage school was going so well that I began contemplating acupuncture school next, but then my plans suddenly shifted. One of my best friends, Brian Balasia, whom I had known since we were both in the womb, started a technology company and asked me to join him in getting it off the ground. I agreed to work for free for a while until the company was more stable. To make ends meet, I returned to power washing and sealing decks, a business that I ran off-and-on for over 10 years and that sustained me through high school and college summers. It was my cousin's husband, Michael, who trained me and helped me grow these entrepreneurial roots. I looked up to Michael—he had a wife, four kids, money in the bank—all the things I wanted someday. His mentorship really shaped me, again revealing to me the power of connection to change a person's life.

After six months of pro bono work, Brian was ready to hire a non-engineer to the team. I was definitely not an engineer, so I was perfect for the job! I came on as a sort of hybrid human resources and project manager extraordinaire. I went back to school to earn a graduate degree in information systems from Walsh College so I could keep up with all of our techies! Over the next five years, the company really took off, growing from 3 team members to 30 in that short time period. We were able to secure a few million dollars of investment from Detroit-based foundations that focused on fostering entrepreneurship and economic growth in Detroit.

I loved the work, but after a few years, I again began to feel a draw to be more connected to people through all of the things I had learned and experienced. I wanted to find a unique way to marry my education in psychology and neuroscience with the exposure to technology I was getting at my job. Something was brewing within me, but I didn't yet know what it would become. I just knew that I wanted to help people find connection in a unique way.

About this time, I first encountered the early effects of social media. MySpace and Facebook had both come to the market during my college years and were beginning to become more foundational to cultural experiences and expectations. From the beginning, though it was exciting to seemingly connect with so many people, I experienced the flip side of the coin. All that digital connection made me feel more disconnected. I quickly learned that endlessly staring at your ex-girlfriend's MySpace page did not bode well for your mental health. I found that increasing information does not necessarily increase connection. But like everyone else, I was becoming more addicted to the internet.

I began drinking more and becoming depressed, and even then, I knew that my online habits were contributing to my issues. Seeing my ex's perfect new guy and her new life—the one right there on my screen—really did a number on me. It affected my emotional and mood regulation. But the internet also provided other opportunities to treat my disconnection in unhealthy ways. Even though I had such huge student loan debt, I began to spend frivolously on eBay. Curse that "buy now" button!

I was a mess, but I was ready to start pulling myself out of it. From that moment, I knew that my dream of mixing psychology and neuroscience with technology would somehow relate to the explosive growth of the internet. I knew that a field was emerging based on what online presence does to person's actual presence. I even tried my hand at a tech startup called MyMentalSpace. It was designed to help you manage your time and mood online—that is, your "mental space." Mind you, this was before the "like" button. It was designed to connect you to others whom you trusted to keep you accountable in spending less time on sites that robbed you of time or presence. It even tracked what kind of mood different sites caused within you. But it wasn't yet my time, and it never took off.

Still, I couldn't escape the vision growing within me that the internet was going to affect mental health and connection as it continued to evolve, just as it already had in my life. Sometimes, you build things because you desperately need them so badly yourself. My product didn't become a household name, but it did foster within me a heart for advocating for what my friend and fellow advocate Amy Blankson calls *digital wellness*.[1]

The other thing this process did was wake me up a bit, lessening my desire for alcohol and shallow relationships. If I was going to help other people become healthier, I knew it was time to prioritize my own health first. About that time, a work friend set me up on a blind date with her sister. But as it happened, I was committed to going to Vegas with some guys for a bachelor party. I set up the date to happen after the Vegas trip, which felt to me like some last hurrah of my party days before it was time to fully grow up.

The weekend was wild, and on the last night, I was walking into an elevator when my phone rang. It was my younger brother, Kevin. I could tell something was very wrong. He broke the news to me that Michael, the guy who helped me get started in power washing and someone I had looked up to, had died by suicide. As the doors of the elevator began to close, I felt my heart drop to the bottom of my stomach. I was devastated in a way I never thought possible. Michael seemed to have it all and be so happy, so I couldn't wrap my mind around what had happened.

Looking back, that time of intense grief and confusion shook me to my core. But it also forged an even deeper desire within me to be mindful and helpful in the mental health space—for myself and for all the Michaels out there. My bet is that you have your own story of knowing someone suffering from mental health issues in some way. Maybe you yourself fight the ill effects of depression, anxiety, or emotional dysregulation.

You are not alone. I share these stories because as I launch into more data and research about the issues of our Distracted Age, I want you to know that this isn't just about stats. We all hurt—and I know the feeling myself. So my thoughts aren't meant to just be cutesy aphorisms for TED Talks or meme-worthy axioms. I write these words thinking about Michael—and about you. No, our digital health is not always a matter of life and death, but increasingly, it can be.

So don't walk alone—and as we explore more and more of the nitty-gritty parts of pursuing presence and connection amid the challenges of the Distracted Age, may we keep humans and their hearts at the center of our journey forward. Like smoking, there's more going on than the mere acceptance or sting of socially acceptable behavior. Even if we don't yet fully realize it, what we inhale affects the very course of our lives.

We must muster up the mindset to want "nonsmoking" sections in our own lives, places where we give our minds and souls relief. Even before the digital age, people have found creative ways to find their own safe mental spaces.

Nonsmoking (Sacred) Spaces

Remember that random blind date I set up before my Vegas trip? I thought about canceling, but my mother urged me not to do that to some innocent woman. Reluctantly, I agreed to go. This proved to be a pivotal decision shaping the course of my life more than I could have ever imagined. I met Ksenija, my future wife.

Keeping that date was a good call!

Years later, Ksenija and I would have *two* beautiful kids. Susanna Wesley, the woman we are about to meet, however, had *19*! Let that sink in. Even more astounding is the fact that Susanna was one of 25 children herself. That's a lot of peanut butter and jelly sandwiches!

Susanna was born to a huge English family in 1669 CE, not exactly what most of us would consider the "good old days." In fact, it may seem so long ago that it's hard to even fathom a comparison between then and now. No electricity. No cars. And of course, no smartphones.

Yet even without an iPhone or an Android, we can speculate with some accuracy that Susanna Wesley faced as many distractions in the seventeenth and eighteenth centuries as you and I face here in the twenty-first. If you have two kids, take that distraction and multiply it by almost 10!

Tragically, 9 of her 19 children died in infancy. I can't even imagine the pain of such widespread trauma. Besides this, she also lived in a challenging marriage to her husband, Samuel Wesley, a stubborn and unpopular clergyman who tended toward harshness both at church and at home. Samuel was also a terrible manager of money and was put into debtor's prison in 1705, leaving Susanna alone to care for a bustling houseful of young children. Also, their house burned down. Twice. It suffices to say that Susanna Wesley faced difficulty and distraction on a historically unprecedented level.

But Susanna was a person of courage, grit, and wisdom. She was far from perfect, but she kept showing up for her family, personally accepting responsibility for educating each of her individual children. She taught them reading, writing, religion, poetry, and the like. She set aside time every night to spend quality time with each of her individual children (on a rotating basis throughout the week, of course). She respectfully listened to each of their unique and specific needs, dreams, and perspectives, offering insight, correction (she was no pushover), and personalized guidance for their respective paths forward in life.

It would be easy to describe Susanna in nearly legendary terms as if she was simply just better, stronger, or more focused than the rest of us. Perhaps she was, but it is more likely that she simply understood the dangers of distraction and took measures to mitigate it in her crazy life situation. She obviously loved her children more than anything in the world, so she did not consider them the problem. Rather, she knew that constant, unending connection and interaction to even the best and beautiful things in the world can ultimately steal our focus, divide our energies, and disrupt our pulse. It wasn't about the children; it was about acknowledging the nature and needs of our own humanity. She took responsibility not just for her children's education but also for her own mental health.

Again, you don't have to be a person of faith to connect with this specific element of Susanna's life and example. Your story or beliefs may be different, but there is something good to be gained from her story. For Susanna, creating intentional time to be quiet and pray was how she kept her mind and soul rested, sharp, and resilient. Otherwise, who among us wouldn't go mad living only a few days in her life situation?

However, where could a seventeenth-century mother of at least 10 young kids in a small house find privacy or quiet? Every corner of the house was filled. Every floor space accounted for. There was no margin. So, Susannah created her own margin.

If every space was filled, she made herself into the space she needed by pulling her apron over her head. Within that self-made fabric sanctuary around her head, she was able to temporarily shut out the rest of the world—even the good parts. Her children knew that when the apron was over her head, she was not to be disturbed unless there was an emergency. They knew the apron was not an expression of their mother's rejection, but an expression of her love. Her boundaries to stay healthy helped her stay present and able to meet their needs.

In a house filled with the noise and motion, this simple act created a sacred space—a private "tent" of stillness in the middle of chaos. There were no locked doors, noise-canceling headphones, or digital calendars to protect her time. Just an apron and a clear boundary, born from a desperate need to connect with something deeper than the demands of the day. I imagine the sound of footsteps softening as her children noticed the apron rise, a small moment of reverence in a household that rarely paused. It's a picture of what many of us long for: a way to reclaim peace and presence amid the noise of our own lives.

Again, you may not be religious, but Susannah's influence reaches through the centuries in a way you probably recognize. If you've ever sung "Hark! The Herald Angels Sing" at Christmas, then you are experiencing the creativity of one of her children, Charles. He wrote over 6,000 such hymns. He worked alongside his brother, John, to spark one of the most significant movements in modern Christendom: the Methodist Church. In a time when many church leaders, religious national leaders, and large-scale evangelistic efforts were focused solely on conversion (oftentimes by very forceful and unchristian means), the early Methodists dug wells, built schools, and erected clinics and hospitals all over the world. The Wesley brothers taught and led tens of thousands of their followers to notice, empathize, and sacrificially meet the needs of the homeless, the hungry, and the hurting at home and abroad.

And it all began, in some small way, under the quiet shelter of their mother's apron.

In our world of constant noise and endless notifications, maybe we too need an apron—a simple, sacred-to-us signal reminding us and others that it's time to pause, breathe, and reconnect with what matters most. It's hard to smoke under an apron. We must find our own systems that help us stop inhaling the smoke of distraction and isolation.

When we find the quiet, we can be even more mindful of all that threatens to steal our presence.

Reflection

Where in your life are you—or someone close to you—hiding behind the illusion of "fine," and what would it look like to move one step toward honesty and connection?

4 Secondhand Distraction and Mark's Law

> "How we spend our days is, of course, how we spend our lives."
>
> —**Annie Dillard**

In the pages to come, I will share more about the early days of my relationship with my wife, Ksenija. But for now, I want to speak to another specific effect of digital distraction on us. If you're married, have kids, or have a significant other in any way, my guess is you will be able to relate.

As a speaker who travels a lot, whenever I leave for a trip, my wife writes me a card for every day of my trip to encourage me and keep us connected while away. This is a habit she's formed that I'm so thankful for! Her words always encourage me and oftentimes, she writes in a way that speaks to the core of my heart and the need I have in that very moment! But then, oftentimes, when we're together in the minivan driving an hour to my brother's house, the same women who was so present in those notes seems like she's not even there with me—and she's right next to me! That's because since the digital age has come into its own. She is like most people in the passenger seat these days: her tendency is to be on her phone. She takes the extra time to catch up on her digital chores.

Again, I'm not anti-technology or even anti–social media. I'm just pro-health and pro-connection. And in this case, I don't want to ride in the car 12 inches from someone, yet virtually alone. I have to be present and attentive to the journey all around us to keep us safe. The irony is that in these scenarios, the kids in the back seat are usually plugged in, watching a DVD with the in-car entertainment system. Regardless, it does mean we could have this rare moment to be present together with few intrusions.

But if I say anything about her time in Instagram, it comes off to her as if I'm trying to control her. She just wants a little time to catch up because she has been exhausted tending to the needs of our kids and family in a way I can't fully understand. That is fair. And to her defense, it has been said that I am perhaps a high-maintenance husband in the sense of communication. That is, I want all of the communication all of the time. Despite it not being possible, I seem to be fluent in all five love languages, so I can acknowledge that it might be a little overwhelming for the one person with whom I want to endlessly converse, even if she loves my wordiness 90% of the time.

But on my side, I just want her time and energy in a way that says I'm her top priority. It's not that we can't have good conversations as she checks her phone between every third sentence, because we do. And often, she's not even on social media. She's helping our family by starting online orders at Whole Foods or getting more school supplies on Amazon—the time windows for shipping are often narrow, and she's balancing a million things to make it possible for me to have the kind of career I have.

Can you see the legitimate tension of it all? No one is setting out to hurt or dismiss anyone else; it's just the fact that so many of our life tasks now seemingly demand our online presence. Attention can be somewhat divided, but presence, by its definition, cannot. You can't be present in two places at once. It's not necessarily her lack of attention that makes me feel lonely in the car. It's her lack of presence.

This is but one example of secondhand distraction. Because I'm driving, I don't have the luxury to be distracted by my phone. She, however, can scroll away to her heart's content. She's not doing anything wrong and her distraction is seemingly harmless. But like someone smoking next to you in a car, someone being completely distracted next to you in a car also deeply affects you.

The real kicker is when she is looking down on her phone and then looks up to encounter a traffic situation that seems sudden to her, but I've seen coming a mile way. She thinks we're not going to stop in time as if that line of cars ahead of us just magically appeared when she looked up from her phone. "Mark! Slow down and watch what you're doing!" The truth is, sometimes I am tailing people and need to slow down, but most of the times, she's not seeing the whole road situation in front of us. When we're distracted, we see only in panicked inches, not in present-minded miles.

I hear stories like this from thousands of people—and my bet is that you're chuckling a bit to yourself because such interactions in the digital age happen on the regular. Secondhand distraction is real. We don't have to be directly distracted ourselves to be affected by distraction. And to be clear, this exact scenario sometimes plays out with Ksenija and me trading places. Sometimes, I'm head's down in the digital world of work or even social media and she calls me on the phone to check in on our day. Nothing critical, just connection. As she shares something small, but still important enough to share in this moment of her day, it doesn't take long for her to notice that despite my "yeahs" and "no ways," I'm not really present in the conversation. She is now experiencing my secondhand distraction.

When we're the ones plugged into another world on our phones, everything feels justified. Our "i-Drenaline" is coursing through our brains and bodies, rewarding us for scrolling in ways our conscious selves may not be able to detect without doing the work required to awake to the parameters of human connection. Even if we're working or doing something for the family, the distraction can still be harmful to ourselves and to those around us.

For the most part, effective multitasking is a myth—trying to divide your true presence among multiple places only leaves you stretched to the extremes. It also affects those around you. The current boundaries of scrolling around each other at the dinner table, on dates, at family events, or in public spaces may be socially acceptable for the moment, but they are actually just digital smoking sections. Before the sharp decline of acceptance of smoking, restaurants would promote designated sections for smokers—and often, they were only a few feet away from the nonsmoking section. It was absurd, but it was acceptable; that is, until we all woke up to the absurdity and agreed it should not be.

We've all felt it when the smoke of secondhand distraction wafts into our face. It's irritating, at best. If someone were to accidentally blow actual cigarette smoke directly into your face, both parties would probably admit that you have a right to be frustrated. Despite smoking section signs, no one has ever posted signs reading, "Don't Blow Smoke into Other People's Faces." Somehow, we are all capable of accepting such boundaries instinctively without offense. But when it comes to digital distraction, we're not there yet. It is offensive and hurtful to ask someone to get off their phone and be present because their secondhand distraction is affecting you as well. Can you see how we've yet to really accept the true realities of how we're living, even though our digital ways are currently acceptable to society?

The phone isn't bad, but secondhand distraction certainly is.

Margin and Mark's Law

Moving from undergraduate work in psychology and neuroscience to a master's program in information systems provided me with a unique lens through which to study the effects of technology on our mental health and social connections. In one of my classes, we learned about a guy named Gordon Moore. In 1965, Moore developed what became known as Moore's law—not the most innovative name, but truly an innovative concept. Moore was the cofounder of a little company called Intel.

Moore's law is an observation that states the number of transistors on microchips will double approximately every two years, which means computing power roughly multiplies at these same regular intervals.

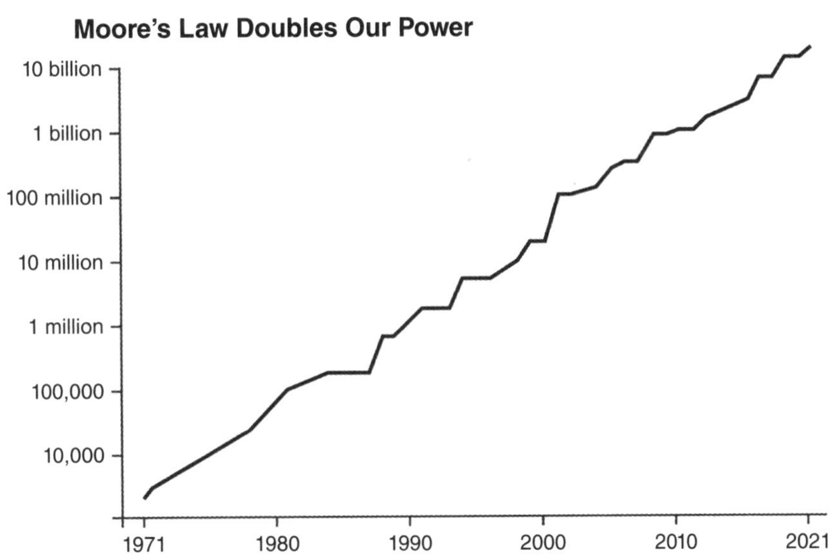

Moore's law: Every two years, the number of transistors per microprocessor doubles.

Data source: Karl Rupp, Microprocessor Trend Data (2022).

In other words, computing power will double every two years as it also continues to decrease in price. (To be clear, someone should probably tell Apple that this doesn't mean they need to completely redesign the power adapters for our computers every two years.)

But all joking aside, Moore's law has maintained its validity for decades and has been a driving force behind rapid technological advancement—from personal computers to smartphones to artificial intelligence (AI). But these days, there are questions about whether Moore's law can keep up with the ever-increasing rapids of our digital society.

As Moore's law struggles to keep up with the forceful advance of the digital age into our daily habits and connections, the result is a marked decline in margin from our lives. One of my favorite authors, Richard Swenson, first used the term *margin* in this way. Swenson was a physician who got fed up with writing endless prescriptions for people who were stressed, burnt out, and overwhelmed, so he decided to devote his life to researching burnout.

Swenson's book, aptly named *Margin*, basically says we each have a "load"—that is, all of our responsibilities and our commitments to which we have constructed our lifestyle and priorities. These are the things we have the ability to do. What remains after them is our margin—extra time and space in the human experience that most people throughout history have experienced in some way. I don't mean to say that enslaved or oppressed people working all day had more time than us. Rather, from the moment they awoke to the moment they fell asleep, their bodies may have been working, but their minds weren't being constantly overstimulated in the way our minds are. Most of us are living marginless lives.

If life is a bank account, it is now common to live in the overdraft. This means that all the essential energy in our inner accounts is constantly being spent and depleted until we're in the red. This leaves very little for the inner life that grows and flourishes with the proper amount of margin and space to sustain it. When we've completely spent ourselves, we become overdrafted and burnt out.

We are overdrafted as a society. Statistically, at present, if we live to be 80 years old, most of us will spend 21 of our years on this earth with our minds on another digital planet.[1] That is, we will spend 21 years behind a screen. But then I thought of Moore's law and the doubling that happens every year. This inspired what I call *Mark's law*. (Creative, right?)

Mark's law states that our attention span is reduced two seconds every 10 years, which could bring us to a place where presence becomes nearly extinct by 2040.

Mark's Law Demands Our Presence

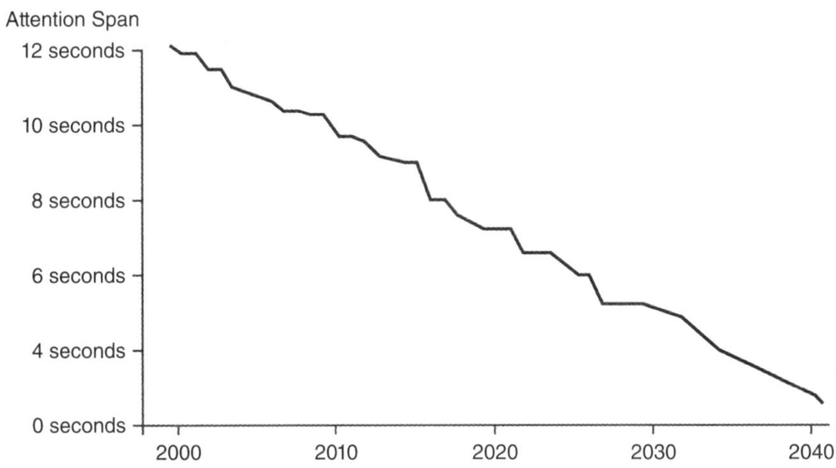

Mark's law: Every decade, we lose about two seconds of attention on a single task.

Some might say it's already happening, but I believe it could become much worse. More and more innovations will emerge promising better multitasking ability or equipping us to be even more passive and noninvasive in real relationships—that is, shallow and hollow to avoid the conflict and discomfort that inevitably comes with being focused on true human connections. On the flip side, online vitriol will continue to be normalized, further dehumanizing our interactions. All this as we simultaneously build and obsess over our digital prowess to no true helpful end. If we don't course correct, our relationships and communities could eventually lack any semblance of real, messy, human presence.

Mark's law is a bummer, isn't it? But it doesn't have to be this way. I also believe in Mark's hope!

Back in 2019 before the pandemic and before Haidt's *The Anxious Generation* had really moved this topic of the dangers of our digital lives down the road, I delivered a TED Talk called "Our Digital Life in 2034—The Rise of Digital Hippies aka 'Dippies.'" Using imagination to project us into the year 2034, I hypothesized what the future could be if someone decides to swim upstream against Mark's law. I theorized that a subset of our population will rise up to say, "Peace, love, . . . and flip phones" (or no phones at all). Whether or not they will wear bellbottom jeans is yet to be determined.

Why would Dippies emerge in our society? Think about the year 2034. By then, these kids-turned-adults will have watched their friends, parents, grandparents, coaches, teachers, leaders, and influences become detrimentally distracted and mentally ill as a result of years of "smoking" digital cigarettes. They will simply say, "We can't do it like this anymore. We want to live."

The Dippies are not yet a fully established tribe, but the movement toward this way of thinking is already underway. But before we get too excited about the idea of a future generation returning to flip phones, we need to acknowledge one critical factor shaping humanity's relationship with technology: we are terrible at predicting its impact in the short term.

A helpful illustration comes from the film *The 8-Bit Christmas*. Set during the year the Nintendo was first introduced in the United States, the story follows a 10-year-old boy whose Christmas dream is to receive a Nintendo from Santa Claus. The tension arises when parents become overly concerned about the potential effects of video games on children's brains and behavior. One memorable scene depicts parents protesting outside retail stores in the streets of Chicago, holding signs that read "Video Game Over," as if video games themselves could and should be stopped forever.

Of course, we know how the story turned out. That 8-bit Nintendo was merely the beginning of decades of gaming innovation, fueled by Moore's law and exponential computing power. What once seemed dangerous or frivolous evolved into immersive, near-lifelike experiences made possible by advanced graphics, processing speed, and virtual reality.

The movie captures this tension beautifully and sets the stage for another helpful concept: Amara's law. It says that we tend to overestimate the effect of a technology in the short run and underestimate the effect in the long run. Roy Amara was a Stanford futurist and former president of the Institute for the Future. He was right about our underestimate of the long-term effects. Technology didn't steal our attention overnight. It slowly trained us to give it away.

We overestimated smartphones at launch, treating them like little more than cool gadgets, while underestimating their lasting impact on attention, anxiety, presence, and childhood. We did the same with social media, celebrating it as a tool for connection, while failing to see how easily it could become a replacement for real human connection. Now AI sits in the same tension. We overestimate its immediate impact through hype and fear, while once again underestimating how profoundly it may shape identity, trust, work, and creativity in the years to come.

The hope is that we don't have to keep going in the direction we're going. We don't have to wait until 2034. We can begin making healthier decisions now, but that will only occur if we fully educate ourselves on what is happening in the world around us, and how it is affecting the world within us. We just need to remember this. Moore's law doubles our power, but Mark's law demands our presence.

But we can only have such presence if we remain awake to three things that threaten to steal it: progress, perception of reality, and pain.

Reflection

Who in your life might feel the effects of your secondhand distraction, and what is one small way you could show them they are your priority this week?

5

The Three Thieves of Presence

> "The ability to sit quietly and think is one of the most valuable skills you can develop."
>
> **—Brian Tracy**

If Mark's law holds true, then presence will be one of the greatest gifts we can offer. Which begs the question, what keeps stealing it? The truth is, most of us are not losing our presence in one dramatic moment, but in small, repeated ways we have come to accept as normal. The speed of progress trains us to live hurried. Our distorted perception of reality keeps us anxious and reactive. And our pain, when left unattended, tempts us to numb rather than heal. Together, these three thieves quietly rob us of margin, clarity, and connection, leaving us physically here but inwardly far away. To reclaim presence, we must first unpack the three thieves of presence.

Thief 1: Progress

If you've ever been to a movie, an office, or have ever just heard some kid on your street revving his old pickup truck with no muffler, then you know that human-made things are rarely quiet. Airplanes rarely sneak up on anyone, neither do power drills, though all of these are signs of human advancement. The sheer progress of the modern life robs us of the quiet, thus it robs us of presence.

In *Margin*, Richard Swenson illustrates the dramatic rise of progress through a set of simple, yet striking graphs. Each one shows how the pace and scale of modern life have accelerated exponentially, much faster than our emotional, relational, or spiritual capacity to keep up. Healthcare costs have taken off like a rocket ship as our populations continue to battle chronic illness.

Healthcare Costs

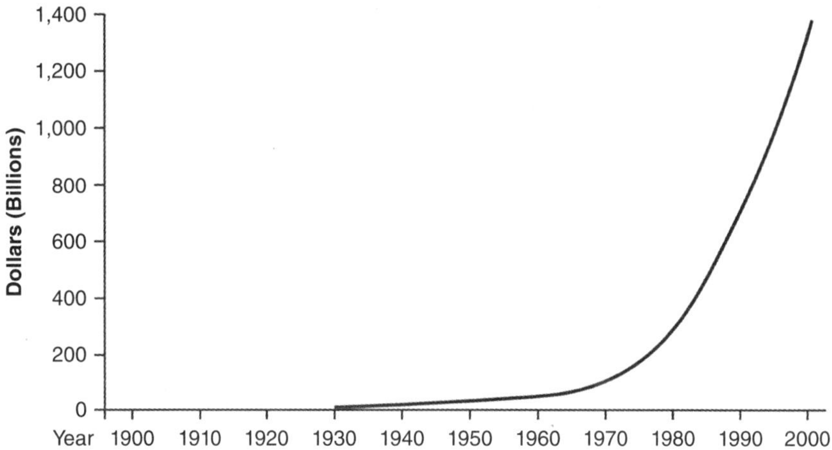

Retail mall square footage per capita has exploded, signaling our shift toward consumption and 24/7 availability. The number of prisons built over the past several decades has risen dramatically, revealing deeper social and cultural divisions than we'd like to admit.

Number of Prisoners: State and Federal

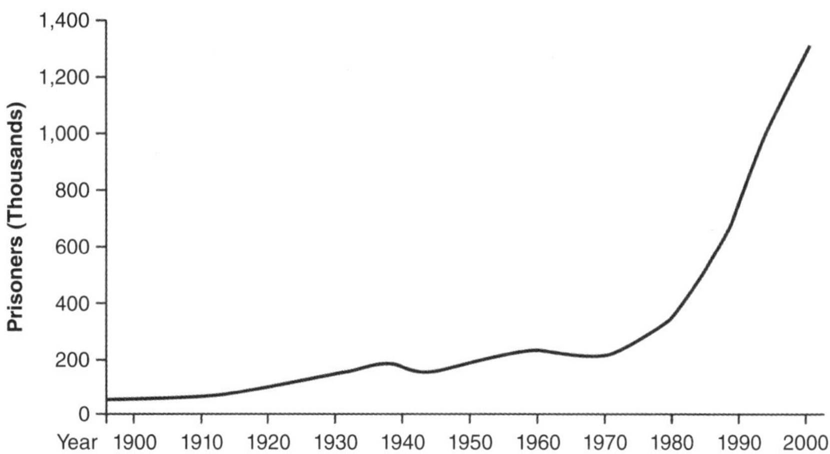

The average American home has nearly doubled or tripled in size (despite the rise in home prices), even as the average size of American families has declined, reflecting a drift toward more possessions and more complexity to manage even among the rise of home prices.

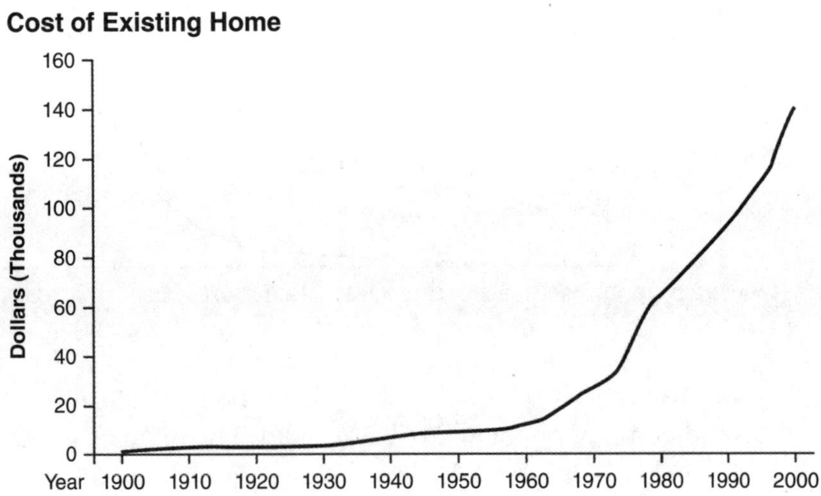

Bankruptcies have soared as financial pressure has intensified, and the volume of advertising has multiplied into an overwhelming river of noise competing endlessly for our attention.

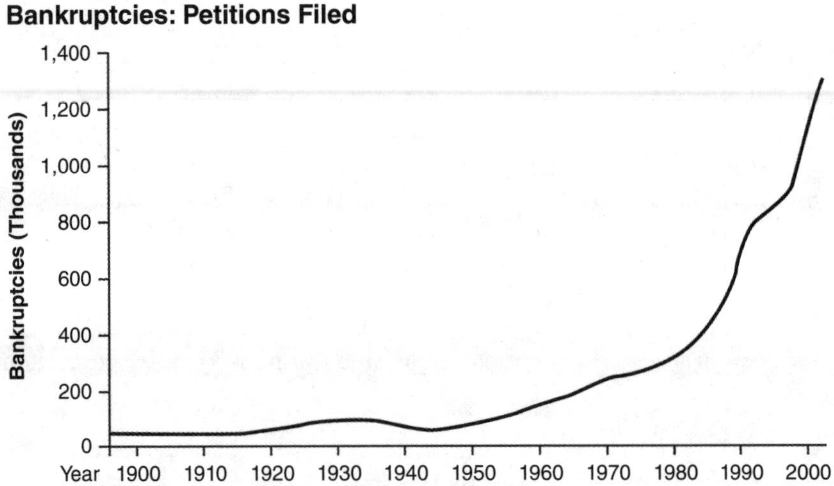

Volume of Advertising

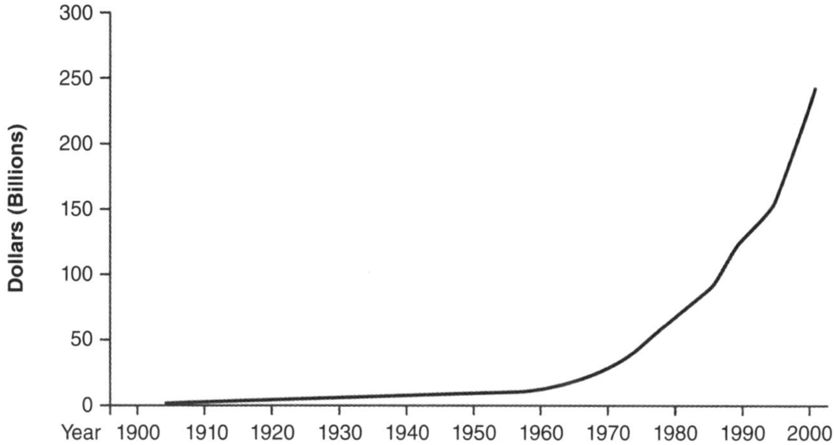

Finally, try to wrap your head around this: we deliver more packages in 2025 in a single day than were delivered in an entire year in the 1970s. Of course, we didn't have the internet in the 1970s; however, even over the past five years, we've seen package shipping explode as our daily needs often live inside a brown box with a smile on it.

Growth of US Package Shipments (1975–2025)

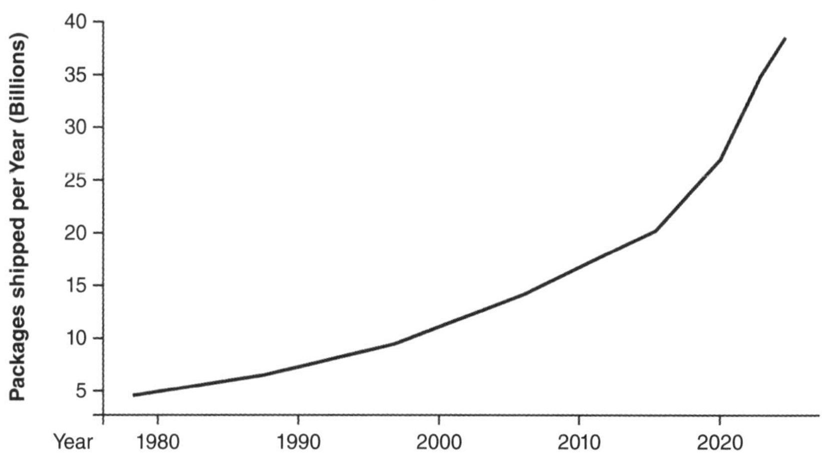

Together, these facts and graphs compose a sobering narrative: progress has accelerated in every direction—well, every direction except the ones that foster and sustain human margin, meaning, and connection.

We once thought that the modern life would have the opposite effect. In 1965, *Time Magazine*'s cover featured a hard-to-describe image of a massive supercomputer, complete with multiple arms and hands doing everything from typing to making phone calls to feeding its own computer mouth with data sheets. There was a huge brain behind the computer monstrosity and scientists gathered at its feet to read and process endless amount of paper data, no doubt indicative of the massive wealth of knowledge (and money) that the computer would make for its masters.[1]

In many ways, the accompanying article was prescient as the computer has indeed filled the modern world with endless amounts of knowledge and profit—and the brain is almost eerily predictive of AI.[2]

But in other ways, they missed it by a country mile.

The writers predicted that computers and automation would eventually lead us into a 24-work-week year.[3] The logic made sense at the time. If computers can do all of this extra labor for humans, then humans would not have to do as much labor for themselves, right? And if we didn't have to work so much, that would leave time for play or "leisure." A leisure class would emerge because people who would have so much free time on their hands that they would spend it as "downtime"—that is, resting, relaxing, and exploring (and experiencing) the adventures of the outside world.

In some ways, they were right. We do have a lot of downtime, but we don't spend it doing things that bring us rest, relaxation, or adventure in the outside world. Instead, we reenter the very world that we thought computers would free us from. Instead of computers affording us the chance to pursue what humans have always dreamed of, they have changed our dreams. Instead of sunsets and adventures, we'd rather sit in the bed and stare at more computers.

Currently, as I write these words, multiple headlines compete for my future-casting energy. The first reads, "Microsoft to Pursue

Superintelligence After OpenAI Deal." Just two weeks ago, another headline ricocheted through the tech world: "800+ Tech Leaders Demand AI Superintelligence Ban." Two starkly different visions of the future surfaced within a two-week span. My friend Amy Blankson points out that "while AI is accelerating at a breakneck pace, the most important story right now is not about machines. It's about us—what we value, what we protect, what we design toward, and what we refuse to outsource." Not only do I agree but I also can't help but think that the thief of progress had something to do with it.

As computers got faster and faster, instead of seeing their advancement as the opportunity to unplug, we have tried to keep up. Compared to our ancestors, we are the leisure class. But the name is misnomer because even if we're not being productive, our brains are still working overtime shifts trying to keep up with the endless scrolling. We think it's leisure, but we feel more tired after doing it in so much excess. The world was supposed to be so much bigger and more accessible, but we made the world we want the most much smaller and all-consuming. We could be a true leisure class, but we choose the opposite. We choose to overwork our minds.

Author and New York University professor Adam Alter "categorizes our screen obsession as a behavioral addiction: 'the drive to engage in an immediately rewarding behavior despite negative long-term consequences for physical, mental, social or financial well-being.'" In other words, we tend to trade what's best for us over time for what's interesting to us in this moment. The leisure class is addicted to overworking our brains. "Examples include gambling, binge-watching, and compulsive social networking. Crucially, behavioral addictions are driven by experiences rather than substances." Alter identifies three key experiences that keep us addicted to these patterns: the removal of stoppage cues, feedback, and goals.[4]

Stoppage cues tell your brain that it's time to take a break. You finish a book. The episode ends. The song concludes. However, the frenetic nature of our modern media, social or otherwise, has intentionally removed these cues. This is why if you're listening to Spotify, it always starts a new song when the current one ends. Or if you're watching Netflix, it will start the next episode before you can even get up and go to the bathroom. **Not stopping has become our default state of mind and engagement—and now we can't stop not stopping.**

Our digital life experiences are also addicting because they provide constant feedback. Much like the digital pulse, we feel the compulsion to engage so that someone on the other end will know we're alive and here in a shared experience. The thing is, we're usually sharing experiences with bots, not people. But getting likes, in-game bonuses, or moving timer dials that promise the next video will play soon—these keep us engaged for hours. We keep engaging because we help but wait for the next kernel of feedback.

Finally, the digital world harnesses an internal driver left over from the reason we created computers in the first place: to reach greater and higher goals. Again, the real purpose was to let computers do work that enabled us to achieve life goals outside of the digital world—quality time with our families, creative endeavors, or grand adventures out in the world. Imagine how much time we would have to reach life goals that no generation before us could have conceived of!

In fact, Cal Newport, author of *Deep Work, Digital Minimalism* and most recently *A World Without Email*,[5] shares that the greatest way to beat tempting distracting behaviors on your phone is to have clear long-term goals. When we're constantly scrolling and checking emails, our brains' reward centers are overrun with short-term rewards. But when we introduce long-term goals, our brains focus on them instead, short-circuiting the addictive tendency to seek only small bursts of dopamine.

That drive has driven us into the ground. Developers and content creators know we are driven by goals, so they put them into every facet of the digital experience. Social media campaigns promise a certain number of likes for a certain price—and we sit and stare at the number rising toward its goal. Even fitness apps can become addictive, though in a better way. I've known people who love to run, but love more to get their daily 10,000 steps in. Breaking a Snapchat streak is a cardinal sin for Gen Z—they will riot over it (gamification at work, my friends).

All of these have driven us to maintain the breakneck velocity normalized by a very abnormal way of life. We've become so accustomed to the noise and speed of progress we no longer think it odd that rarely do quiet spaces exist around us, much less within us. One of the first modern motivational speakers to emerge in the 1980s was Brian Tracy. He suggested that the best way to gain clarity when facing a big decision is to sit in utter silence for 30 to 60 minutes with no coffee, no music, and no phone. As he writes, "the answer to your biggest problem will come to you, almost like a butterfly alighting on your shoulder."[6] Out of this quiet space, the modern pace of expected progress slows to a pace that enables your mind to rest, affording the best option room to reveal itself. Could you imagine if we all committed to such a practice?

Unfortunately, we do the opposite—and so the speed of progress keeps us from slowing down and keeps our brains aflutter in fight, flight, or freeze mode. There are unintended consequences to this way of being, many of which were unforeseen by the likes of *Time Magazine* in 1965, including our skewed perception of reality.

Thief 2: Perception of Reality

In September 2018, 26-year-old Arthur Medici tragically died from a great white shark attack in Cape Cod. It was the first fatal shark attack in over 80 years. But even though no one had died in such a manner since 1936, in the digital age, the reverberation was so much greater that Boston University wrote an article about its possible effects on the tourism industry the following summer. The death was tragic, but the truth is, you're "more likely to be crushed by an office vending machine than to die by a shark attack."[7]

What made the public perception so juxtaposed to reality? According to Questrom School of Business professor Carey Morewedge, "[Since] shark attacks are emotionally evocative, tourists will probably overestimate the risk of experiencing" one. We react the deepest to what moves us the most. People "perhaps base their choice of vacation location on this kind of risk," Morewedge continued, "while neglecting riskier kinds of activities that are less evocative, but even more dangerous—like the amount of driving they will do to get to their vacation."[8] But there was more to it than just the nature of the event.

Prospective vacation swimmers became tentative about bringing their families to Cape Cod after a celebrity surfer warned people away on social media. Furthermore, the *Boston Globe*'s travel columnist suggested that travelers avoid the "the bloated, shark-happy Cape."[9] The only thing more dangerous than a great white shark to the Cape's tourism industry was the great digital post. Nowadays, what is posted becomes more valid than what is real.

In the era of misleading news and emerging "bot news," it's getting even harder for media outlets to report the truth, even when they have good intentions. Even back in 2006 before the digital age had fully taken root, the Sago Mine disaster in West Virginia became a national lesson in the differences between perception and reality. After an explosion trapped 13 miners underground, early reports by the *Charleston Gazette* that were amplified by outlets announced that 12 of the men had been found alive. Communities celebrated, families rejoiced, and the country exhaled in relief. But the headline was wrong. In the chaos, misinformation and unverified reports spread faster than the truth could catch up. Tragically, only one miner survived. The gap between what people believed and what was actually happening revealed just how quickly perception can take on a life of its own, especially when hope, emotion, and media pressure collide.[10]

Another example I see in our friends' group involves parents who, by algorithmic design, daily feed on a balanced diet of fear and trembling. One good friend shared that when her four-year-old son had a bad fever, she Googled "causes of high fever" and spiraled into endless pages of WebMD. She temporarily believed her son had lymphoma, which was not true. Deep down inside, she knew she was trapped in a mirage of motherly misdiagnosis, but she felt like she couldn't help herself.

Perception has always shaped people's reality, but never has perception been so easily skewed. I think it's a result of so much i-Drenaline coursing through our veins. We are conditioned to gravitate to the extreme and sensational—and these rarely pair well with being present and healthy. We catastrophize much easier than ever before in history—after all, the internet constantly draws our eyes to catastrophes, real and imagined. Pretty soon, we come to expect the worse when, oddly enough, we don't have the "comfort" of our devices to tell us what the worst might be. The delivery mechanism of our greatest insecurities has itself become our greatest security—a false security, to be clear.

I call this *cliff thinking*. A prime example comes to mind from our early days of parenting. One day, Ksenija and I left the house to pick up some diapers from Target. This was early in the iPhone days, so back before social media had really taken hold as the default reality of false community and expression. Even so, the possibilities that the phones provided were already affecting us profoundly.

I pulled out of the driveway and drove us two blocks down the road when Ksenija suddenly said, "I forgot my phone! Let's turn around and go get it."

Being new to the phone phenomena, I innocently said, "Eh, you're fine. We'll just be gone for like an hour. Don't worry about it."

If you've been married for any amount of time, then you know how certain words and phrases spoken within the bounds of matrimony tend to be heard and interpreted in their opposite form. "Calm down" is the primary example. Go ahead, tell your husband and wife to calm down and let me know what happens. "Why did you do that?" is another prime example. It sounds like we're concerned that our significant other just ran into a wall for no reason, but it is interpreted quite differently on their end. And as I found out that day, "don't worry" also fits the bill because despite my kind directive, worry is exactly what she did.

"But what happens if my parents need to get a hold of us?" she asked.

I was now determined not to turn the car around because this seemed ridiculous. I rolled my eyes at her, another stellar marriage maneuver that always produces the desired result. "Uh, I think they will just call my phone, you know?"

From a logical place, she did know. But what she was experiencing wasn't logical; it was emotional. It was cliff thinking. The closer we got to Target, the more her anxiety and frustration kept building. I could feel it on my side of the car.

Finally, the dam burst. "Mark, turn the car around. I need to get my phone."

Now I was becoming genuinely worried about her. "Ksen," I said gently, "it's okay. I've got my phone right here. Your parents are fine."

Tears filled her eyes. "But what happens if my dad gets sick?" To me, it was coming out of nowhere, but now I can see that without her tangible source of insecurity, she was being drawn to all the worse scenarios that she might miss without it. The fear of the unknown was pushing her closer and closer toward the cliff, even though the phone didn't actually assuage such fears. It just made her feel like it did.

"Sweetie," I said, "I was just with your dad last weekend having coffee at the house. He's doing great and taking good care of himself."

As we approached the turn for the Target parking lot, she was in a full panic. "But, Mark! What if my dad dies?" Boom. She had jumped off the cliff. As irrational as it seemed, physiologically, her body was producing its own adrenaline trying to make up for the fact that her phone wasn't causing i-Drenaline to course through her veins. Her mind had become a vacuum of worry. We were only a few minutes away from her phone, but in her mind, she needed that rectangular life force to stay connected to the what-if situations created by the i-Drenaline pumping through her body.

My wife is one of the most secure people I know, so if this sounds a little much to you, I encourage you to stop and ask yourself, "When was the last time I left the house without my phone?" This isn't about security or strength. It's about our addictive need to have our phone on our person at all times because it so greatly affects our perception of reality, even if it's a reality that isn't truly real.

But it *feels* real enough to rob us from being present in this current moment. Our minds have become conditioned not to look around at the life we have, but to look downward at the life that could be, whether good or bad. Instead of living it, it keeps us trapped in a very specific, very curated version of life's story, both of ours and others.

Thief 3: Pain

As you remember in my own story, I never felt so low as that moment I heard the news that Michael had committed suicide. It devastated me in new ways. Pain will do that—uncover new parts of your inner self you never knew existed by making you hurt in ways you never thought possible. Thankfully, I listened to my mom and went on that blind date, even though I felt like a shell of a man.

Little did I know, but my moment of deepest pain led me to the person with whom I would have the deepest connection. Ksenija didn't reject me for hurting—the people who love you well don't work that way. She actually had an understanding of the pain I was feeling. She was three years older, which in terms of wisdom in your twenties, can feel like more. I felt lost, but she had empathy and discernment to help me find my way. She invited me to her church and also helped me get back into counseling. Ksenija also encouraged me to let go of my unprofitable business startup and instead, she encouraged me to pursue speaking and writing. Out of my greatest pain, I suddenly found my greatest purpose and a new lease on life.

Six months into dating, we heard an incredible message at a non-denominational church about why relationships fail. A gifted pastor named Steve Norman was teaching a series on reality TV and how it connects back to the Bible. In one particular service we attended, he showed clips from the show *The Bachelor.* I will never forget as this good-looking guy watches a dozen size-zero women climb out of a limousine and approach him to flirt and attempt to win his approval and affection. By the second date, he's making out with a few of them. By the third date, he's on a helicopter ride in Costa Rica, thinking about proposing to one of them.

At that point, the pastor stopped the video and asked, "Guys, is this what it's like to date in our culture?"

The advent of the digital age was beginning to normalize things like *The Bachelor,* not-so-slowly reshaping our perceptions of relational reality. In that moment as we pondered what fosters true, deep connection, I realized I was holding the hand of the woman I was going to marry. I thought about what brought us together—and I can tell you, it was not a limousine or a helicopter hot tub. (Those are a thing, right?)

No, it was refusing to hide from pain rightly expressed so that trust could be built on a solid foundation. Ours wasn't a relationship poured and gelatinized in the mold of the world's alternate digital reality. Jell-O's great and there's always room for it, but it can't stand up under any kind of pressure. It will jiggle down to nothing in a heartbeat. Rather, our relationship came to being in the fires of adversity, honesty, and empathy.

Pastor Steve showed a visual of a pyramid that represented that core elements of any relationship.[11] Physical attraction was at the very top of the pyramid, with ever-enlarging segments moving downward as they got bigger. Physical connection was built on emotional understanding, which was built on a psychological knowing, which was built on a spiritual foundation at the very bottom.

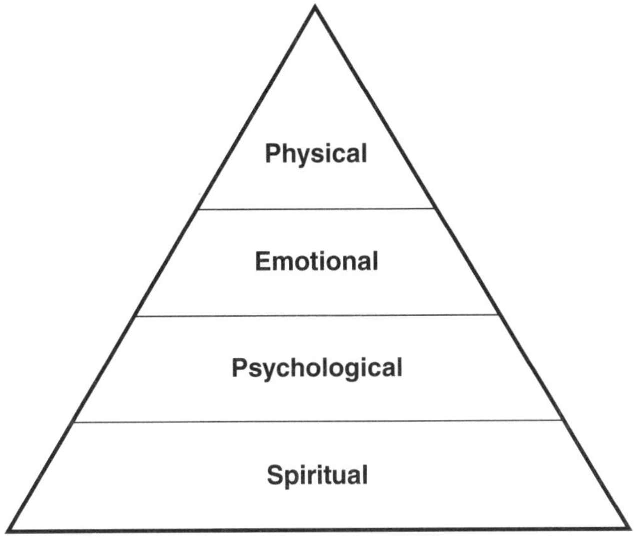

In the West and in my life, I realized that we tend to try to build our relationships primarily on physical and digital connections. It's an upside-down pyramid—a Jell-O pyramid, if you will. It's trying to balance things on the tip of the physical connection, so everything comes tumbling down.

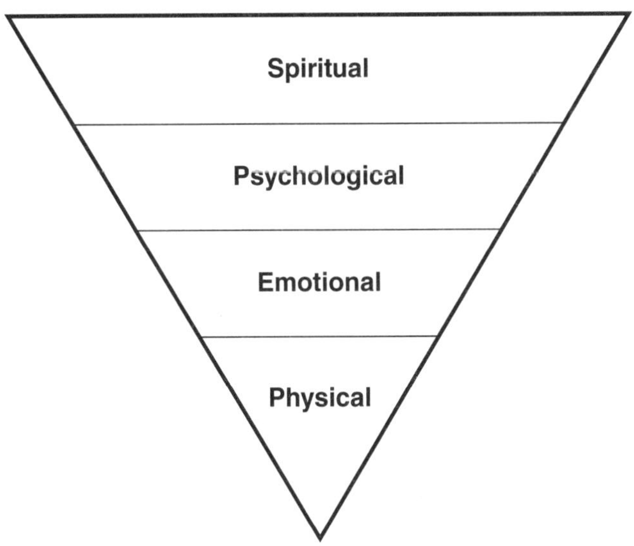

There was enough history from my own story to know that such an approach wasn't yielding the life I wanted. Ksenija and I committed to continuing to build our connection, family, and even intimacy on the foundation of our faith, something higher than ourselves and stronger than the superficial connections offered in an alternate universe like world of *The Bachelor*, no matter how normalized it has become.

We were baptized six months later. I began connecting more deeply with my truest self through sobriety, therapy, and just living my new life as a faith follower. The pain was still there, but it began to have purpose—and it propelled me into an authentic desire to help other people see the gift they are. Rightly aligned, pain helped me find a deeper sense of presence in a real life.

But if we're not careful, our approach to dealing with pain can produce the opposite effect: it can rob us of presence. I believe that our incessant scrolling is a by-product of emotional drifting, like someone on a pool float being pulled out to sea by a growing storm. Who would do such a dangerous thing? Why do we choose to drift? We drift because we don't want to deal with the pain inside. Maybe we've tried and it seems like it didn't work. So instead of facing the storm, we just get on our phone-shaped floats and let the undertow pull us wherever it will.

We've all been there. Bored during a board meeting, you look at your phone under the table and drift into the shallows of sports headlines and Candy Crush. There's no one to hang out with on a Friday night, so in your isolation, you lie in the bed, scrolling for six hours to pass the time and the pain of loneliness. Of course, though you may chuckle out loud a few times at TikTok videos, you're only seconds away from a familiar exhaustion and depression because somewhere deep down inside, the unattended-to pain of your loneliness is robbing you of presence.

Scrolling cannot heal our pain. In fact, scrolling literally does the same thing to our brains as slot machines according to Tristian Harris, a Silicon Valley insider and featured subject of the hit Netflix documentary, *The Social Dilemma*.[12] You may not be completely opposed to gambling, but my bet is you would never advise someone dealing with deep emotional pain to pony up all their life's savings to spend a few days blowing off steam in a casino. We all know that legitimate inner pain cannot be healed by superficial distractions, especially harmful ones. No, relief and health for the inner life requires some sort of care related to the inner life.

This isn't an anti-technology viewpoint; it is just a realistic reflection on the way our lives work in the real world, which includes our inner world. We need to cultivate an inner life that grows in strength. We need practices that lead to inward stillness and peace. We need sacred spaces that invite reflection and introspection in the middle of our crazy day-to-day existence. This inner place is where we can be honest with ourselves about things that need to change in our attitudes, words, and behaviors. Why? Because we can more clearly see our true selves when we are untethered and unclouded from our so-called digital existence. We can see the paths that lead to peace, effectiveness, and fruitfulness.

Your pain hurts—and I'm truly sorry that it does. I'm not belittling your suffering. I know firsthand how a heart can ache and break. I join you in the human condition. But let me encourage you with truth you may hear online, but that you can't internalize purely by online means: being in pain is not a reason to trade the pursuit of a healthy inner life for the numbing of a digital one.

But numbing is our go-to way of being. Why else does the average person now spend four and a half hours a day on their phone—and I mean outside of work? If our phones were treadmills, our fingers move five miles a day. Could you imagine how much better you would feel if your legs jogged five miles a day? Your fingers have the opposite effect. The online world is a treadmill—you work hard, but you never get anywhere. We senselessly scroll the mileage of a marathon every week, which is why people in difficult seasons can get stuck for so long. They're churning, but not moving. The same rings true for relationships in which people feel trapped or lost in, as it also does for jobs in which people feel inadequate and complacent. When the digital existence is prioritized, we live on a treadmill.

I know the feeling. We've all felt internally stuck. If you've lost your job, hours of scrolling on LinkedIn for the next job is probably not going to get you unstuck. It is more likely that calling a friend who used to work at your old agency and asking them for a random lunch is going to pay much better dividends. Scrolling can help you find some opportunities, but eventually, only connection can help you find the next step or sustain the next season.

Likewise, you won't get relationally unstuck trying to win back your ex-boyfriend or ex-girlfriend by posting the best picture of yourself, the one you put 10 filters on after you took 15 selfies on a certain day when you looked your best. That is not going to be as fulfilling as going on a blind date or getting coffee with a friend you met at a party, church, or wedding. Your heart needs people more than it needs mindless activity.

As a society, we're holding onto our pain in ways that keep us from being present with ourselves or others. It is estimated that one in five adults live with diagnosable mental illness. Furthermore, 1 in every 10 people have experienced some kind of traumatic event, whether "big *T*" or "little *T*" trauma. Big *T* trauma can be anything from abuse and physical violence to witnessing the death of a loved one or being abandoned or hurt by an authority figure who should have been safe. But the little *T* traumas also don't need to be dismissed. People face guilt, shame, anxiety, and rejection—and often, they have processed it so poorly over so many years that now it has led to unhealthy beliefs and habits. My wife and I even created a journal to help people grow emotionally and spiritually as we do the same. It's called the Walk Forward Journal and helps people process their pain (Google it).[13]

Poorly processing any kind of pain or trauma throughout our younger years can cause us to grow up with a distorted viewpoint of our adultness. We feel stuck in the patterns that hurt and trapped us as children. We fail to embrace our empowerment and agency.

We feel powerless. We drift. But instead of dealing with it through therapy or working through it with trusted friends, we choose to stay busy with nothingness.

But pain doesn't have to be a thief. It can be a stepping stone to deeper connection. Yes, it has to be with people you can trust and yes, finding those people can be difficult. But even as we actively look for someone to walk with us, we must remember that we cannot ask of the digital world what it cannot deliver. We must keep reminding ourselves of what is real and resist the urge to let scrolling send us into the emotional drift, as if our pain can be pushed out to sea. Pain is never out of sight, out of mind—it always washes back up on the shore in the most inopportune times.

Remember what Susanna Wesley, whom we met in Chapter 3, reminds us with her life: there are always reasons to numb out, embrace distractions, and drift into non-mindful living. But even if all we have is an apron, we have the ability to awaken again today to presence in real life and real connections with real people.

After all, our presence is our gift, if we can only awaken to it.

Reflection

Which thief of presence—progress, perception of reality, or pain—most consistently steals your attention, and what becomes possible when you notice it?

6

Uncertainty Is the Way

"The cave you fear to enter holds the treasure you seek."

—Joseph Campbell

There's nothing like a honeymoon. Even outside of marriage, there's a reason they call it a *honeymoon period*. A new job, project, endeavor, or relationship is fresh out of the gate and running smoothly on even ground. Communication is seemingly easy, not because of seasoned experience, but because not enough time has passed to cross any awkward or difficult bridges. Skies are bright. Emotions are positive. Things feel stable and certain.

Such was my real honeymoon with my new bride. Ksenija and I flew south to Punta Cana in the Dominican Republic. From the outset, everything was perfect. When we arrived, they upgraded us to the honeymoon suite overlooking the beach. The weather was perfect. We laughed. We loved. We ate like kings and queens. In fact, I have this vivid memory of feeling so carefree that one day, we just ordered chocolate cake to the room at noon. It was all-inclusive, so why not?

The cake arrived to the room, covered on a silver tray. I picked up the shiny lid and gazed on the sweet dessert, but suddenly, I lost my appetite. Looking back, I think that things felt too perfect and I knew there was something Ksenija didn't know about me that could derail it all. I had a secret and now that we were married, I had no intention of having my cake and eating it, too. I wanted her to know everything. I felt a compelling conviction to speak up.

I put the lid back on the tray and told her that I really needed to share something, something I had never told her in our two years of dating. A lump formed in my throat and I could tell she was also nervous. This suddenly did not feel like honeymoon talk.

I revealed something I hadn't told anyone. The week before we met when I was on the guys' trip to Las Vegas and where I received the news about Michael's suicide, I had hooked up with a girl I had just met. When I told her about it, I broke down sobbing. I was so scared I was going to blow up our 10-day honeymoon—and who knows, maybe our new marriage. But I also knew that real connection meant I couldn't hold onto such a secret. I wanted to be as close to her as possible, which required the risk of uncertainty.

She knew who I was back then, including my lifestyle of drinking and searching for relationships focused more on physical connection than the other parts needed to foster true intimacy. She also knew I was hurting and grieving the loss of Michael. But even so, I knew she had a right to be angry. Not telling her something that big for so long could have been interpreted as a betrayal. After all, we had built a relationship based on honesty, forgiveness, and the mutual trust growing within our firm foundation of faith. Even though I didn't know her and we weren't together while I was in Vegas, I still felt so convicted to share this with her.

The moment of truth came. To my great relief, instead of pushing me away, she reached over and pulled me into her arms. I had tears in my eyes, so wounded by the thought that I might wound her and lose the one I loved the most in this world. Instead, she embraced me. She held me. She never asked a bunch of questions or demanded an explanation or context. She just wanted my heart in that moment. And I learned firsthand that the truth truly does set you free.

Vulnerable moments don't all have such a happy ending. However, this one taught me about their importance if we are to have any real or meaningful connection. In some ways, the digital world offers the illusion of a perpetual honeymoon. Everyone is dressed and filtered to look their best. Besides the political vitriol, when people share anything about their own lives, they tend to share only what is impressive, endearing, or that otherwise paints them in a positive light.

The problem is, the honeymoon period isn't meant to last forever. It is wonderful and beautiful in a way like no other time, but it is intended to launch people into the unpredictable waters of relationship ahead. It is not the waters themselves. In terms of the nitty gritty details of real marriages, families, and relationships, they are not always comfortable like an all-inclusive resort. However, if they are to grow into strength and stability—the kind that enriches the soul for a lifetime to come—they need to be all-inclusive in terms of trust-based vulnerability.

But the thing about vulnerability or any other key to true connection is that it brings with it a degree of uncertainty. In this way, uncertainty is a necessity to awakening to presence. And uncertainty is never comfortable.

No one sets out to find uncertainty or discomfort. We set out to find something good, significant, or life-giving. But those things are not as readily available as our reels would have us believe. The good things in life that produce purpose and have lasting impact always lie on the other side of the risks of uncertainty and discomfort. They will require courage and vulnerability. They will not be predictable. I had no idea how my new bride might react to my honesty about my past, but I also knew that a walk in that uncertain wilderness was worth what might wait for us on the other side: deeper, authentic, lasting connection built on radical honesty. When we lean into the wilderness of all that we endeavor to avoid in the modern life, we find the very adventure, connection, and presence we most long for.

Just as you can't reach England from the United States without crossing over an ocean in some way, whether by ship or by plane, you can't reach fullness of life and connection without crossing over uncertainty in some way. Difficulty has become the ultimate deterrent to pursuing the best things in life, rather than a necessary element of the pathway leading to them.

Many aphorisms apply here. *No pain, no gain. Nothing ventured, nothing gained. Fortune favors the bold.* Yes, these make great memes, but they speak to a deeper truth being actively lost in meme-based culture. They sound better than they feel, right? Yet we all engage in stories where someone showed up—had presence—in a difficult or uncertain situation, fighting through it for the sake of those they loved or for a cause higher than themselves. No one watches movies on Netflix about someone who never took a risk, faced uncertainty, or braved discomfort—or even danger—to see their lives moved toward something good, beautiful, or worthwhile. Well, I guess the only movies like these that exist are comedies. We tend to laugh at those with no grit or gumption to face the difficulties of life because, deep inside, we know that is not living.

But sometimes the best way to learn how to live is from good old-fashioned wisdom of our forefathers!

Little House on the Prairie

We're very particular about what we watch as a family. We tend to settle on old 1980s and 1990s sitcoms. A little Urkel here and a little Alf there. And while everything in those days was not all wholesome, it is certainly easier to find things that were—and also actually funny and entertaining as well.

We love sitcoms, but nothing has been better for us than an old show that released its first season in 1974: *Little House on the Prairie.* We're currently on the fifth season. The show dramatizes the story of the Ingalls family who migrate west in the 1870s to live on a farm on Plum Creek near Walnut Grove, Minnesota. They are pioneers in a wild place only beginning to develop into a town capable of sustaining families. Theirs is a story filled with difficulty, danger, and uncertainty.

Theirs is also a story filled with deep family and community connection, trust-based vulnerability necessitated by a mutual need to survive, and an expectation of each other's presence—because despite the promise of large tracts of land to work and develop, in the end, they discover that all they really have are each other.

In this second half of my life, I am most inspired by the father figure in the story, Charles Ingalls, played by beloved actor, the late Michael Landon. They call him "Pa" (though it sounds more like "Paw"). Pa Ingalls carries the weight of his family's well-being on his shoulders, while also struggling to make ends meet. The family must live off the land, a difficult and uncertain process, to say the least. Wild animals. Drought. The spread of disease. Danger lurks around every corner.

But does all this difficulty make Pa discontented and angry? Sometimes, but not chronically. The overriding effect of all the uncertainty is that Pa and the family continually experience new depth of gratitude, connection, and presence. They are grateful for every meal on the dinner table and every penny in the jar. Even as Pa is always looking for extra work and is frustrated by the real scarcity he faces, he always turns back to family and his faith.

The household runs in a way that would make most modern families run and hide. The adults and kids are all awake at dawn doing chores and pitching in to help with each difficulty that arises. While I know it is just a television show, I have read enough personal historical accounts to know that the real pioneers from those days displayed a greater sense of grit and a more positive outlook on life than the modern generation. This is not an indictment on the modern generation. People then were not instinctively "better" than people today. I just believe that our avoidance of uncertain and difficult pathways in life in exchange for a seemingly predictable and pleasing appearance of a digital life has robbed us of that which makes us most alive and most present.

Pa Ingall's way of being a man who provides and protects his family is tragically being lost on today's young men. This is not a hypermasculine or toxic masculine take. Women can be protectors and providers, too, but on the whole, the men are struggling to keep up. Young men's way of being in the digital world is hindering their progress in the physical world.

According to professor and author Scott Galloway, 45% of men aged 18 to 24 have never asked a woman out in person. Galloway attributes this change to the rise of social media as what he calls a "rage machine." He also cites the availability of lifelike pornography that eliminates the perceived need for real human connection, as well as a cultural environment where men fear being seen as predatory for expressing romantic interest. The result is a generation of young men increasingly disconnected from the traditional pathways to relationship, family, and purpose. The provider-protector role embodied by figures like Pa Ingalls has become increasingly difficult to fulfill.[1]

Whether male or female, our complacency as a society that keeps us stuck in patterns of online scrolling, rather than physical walking or strolling, has made us addicted to false certainty and comfort. Again, **we walk farther with our fingers than we do with our feet.** And yet emotionally and relationally, we are more miserable than the Ingalls—more discontented than poor people digging their own wells, sewing their own clothes, and suffering through harsh winters with no propane heaters.

In *The Anxious Generation*,[2] Haidt agrees that we need to focus on more independence in raising with our children. They need time away, away from a phone-based childhood and encouragement toward a play-based childhood. My friend and fellow outdoor advocate Ginny Yurich, author of *Until the Streetlights Come On* and host of the award-winning *1,000 Hours Outside* podcast says, "It may shock you to learn that we spend an average of 4–7 minutes outside each day—while we spend 4–7 hours using devices with screens. Needless to say, our physical, mental, emotional, and relational health has suffered. But there is a ready solution: get outside!"[3]

Haidt agrees and shares that kids need to be climbing trees, riding bikes, and coming home before dark as we loosen our grip on the leashes that seek to control their whereabouts 24/7. When we also encourage children to participate in chores and household responsibilities, it boosts their sense of independence and teaches them responsibility. According to Julie Lythcott-Haims, drawing on data from the Harvard Grant Study, professional success in life correlates with having done chores as a child.[4]

One more unique point here about how our pain affects our presence. In 2009, National Center for Biotechnology Information published a study about how dopamine modulates effort-based decision-making in rats.[5] In other words, it was about how the presence or removal of difficulty and uncertainty affects a rat's behavior. They found that if you give a rat a piece of cheese, it releases dopamine. To be clear, if you give me a piece of cheese, it has the same effect. Nothing groundbreaking there.

But they also found that if you place the cheese like four feet away from the rat and add difficulty or challenges between them, like a hurdle or a maze, when the rat finally reaches the cheese, the process of doing so activates other reward centers in its brain, producing even more dopamine. The rat also burns more calories. In other words, it finds more fun in the hunt than in being given the cheese without difficulty or challenge. In fact, when given the choice, the rats chose the large-reward option despite the extra effort required.[6]

The thing is, we've been given a choice as well. Much of our modern life has removed the hunt for our natural reward system. We've never had more cheese and we've also never had to do less work to find it. And yet, we've never felt more disconnected, depressed, and distant. From Pa Ingalls to Papa Rat, we are invited to re-embrace the uncertainty of real life instead of languishing in a false reality that robs us of the gifts of difficulty, which also robs us of the gift of presence.

My own story proved the common expression to be true: uncertainty in life produces the best cheese. Okay, so no one says that, but you get the point.

"Purple Rain" and Unexpected Turns

I mentioned previously that I joined a tech startup that took off. It was a hard path, but at first, things went well. In fact, I stayed there 10 years. But after that initial push, we had run through much of our investment capital and were struggling to make payroll. This led to uncertainty and the difficult decision to lay off half of our staff.

Soon thereafter, our first son was born and I took two weeks of paternity leave. I could have never predicted what happened next: one week into my leave, my best friend—who was also my boss—called me to let me know they had to let me go, too. It wasn't personal. There was just not enough capital. Talk about finding yourself suddenly in the wilderness! All I was missing was a covered wagon!

We had a new baby at home and we needed stability. What was I going to do? Have you ever been there? It was stressful and scary, but at the same time, there was a certain energy underneath it all, the kind you can only feel when you face uncertainty. It was all for one and one for all. We had nothing but God and each other—and there was a thrill to it!

As I began looking for work, a friend asked me if I knew anything about account management. When you're in a comfortable place, you have more margin to weigh and ponder what you think you can and cannot do. But when you're in the Wild West, you just say yes to what's next. I needed a job, so guess what, I suddenly knew how to do account management.

Little did I know that I would spend the next six years of my career at a creative studio called Skidmore in downtown Detroit. It was an incredible experience working alongside 20 of the most creative people I've ever known. I reported directly to the president, Tim Smith. Tim was a great boss, but an even better man. He had a lot of grace for my current season of life because he had two grown children, and by this point, Ksenija and I had two kids.

Tim walked the line between relational connection and business intensity. He was all-in financially on the business side of things and as a result, at times he was emotionally and mentally strapped. I felt a draw to be there for him and help him find balance and presence. Thus, most of our one-on-one lunches were less about developing accounts and selling brand strategy services to our clients and more about larger questions about the meaning of life, managing stress, and this God guy I kept circling back, too. Tim also taught me the power of the word *unbelievable*. He understood how work matters can quickly swing from good to bad, so when people asked, "How's business going," he would simply respond, "Oh, it's unbelievable!" They assumed this meant it was great and wouldn't ask any more questions, even when in reality, things may have been unbelievably bad. Tim was a funny guy.

It was a season of hard work and valuable lessons. It also enabled me to meet quite a few business leaders and influencers in Detroit, including billionaire Dan Gilbert and his large enterprises of the

Cleveland Cavaliers and Quicken Loans, now known as Rocket Mortgage. All told, I spent six years at Skidmore with the expectation that I could begin speaking and writing on the side. I began to develop my clientele, speaking for every Michigan client I could connect with.

It was a time of building bridges, but just like my earlier 10 years in tech, I was exposed to the pain point of small business life, which basically means learning to live month-to-month, if not paycheck-to-paycheck. While there is nothing wrong with pursuing more stability, I became conditioned to the uncertainty, learning that even without a huge and predictable safety net, we would be okay. We didn't have to have all the questions answered or all the boxes checked in order to be secure and content. We just needed to work hard, take the next step, and be present with one another the best we could.

I also continued to learn that connection is the most valuable commodity in any workplace endeavor. As my friendship with Tim grew, I came to know that besides his family, he loved two things: baseball and Prince (or the artist formally known as Prince, or whatever you want to call the guy who wrote "Purple Rain"). Tim owned every Prince album and took his sons to almost every major league baseball stadium in the country. He wanted to live life to the fullest.

His energy spilled over into our workplace culture. I can remember him walking about the office wearing a Mickey Mouse T-shirt, constantly encouraging everybody to be creative and dare to do mighty things. As he began speaking more, he even wrote a book called *Dare Mighty Things*. But two months after his book was released, his heart stopped beating in the middle of a meeting.

Tim was rushed to the hospital, but the prognosis wasn't good. The whole thing shook our entire studio. He was only 54 years old. I got permission from our chief financial officer, Drew, the friend who brought me into the business, to go visit Tim at the hospital during the workday.

When I arrived, Tim's wife and sons had just left, so I found myself alone with him in the hospital. He was unconscious and on medically induced life support. As I looked at him in his hospital gown, I reminisced about the earlier days of our business when we would wear suits to conferences. We were an illustrative shop that had once created illustrations of every car available for purchase from the Big Three (GM, Ford, and Chrysler) in newspapers back in the 1960s and 1970s. At this point in our history, we were designing and selling websites, brands, and logos. It was a really special studio. We created metal pins to give to our clients. Of course, we'd also wear them proudly at conferences and client meetings.

In fact, I had the urge to bring one of those old pins with me to the hospital. As he lay there with tubes coming and going out of his body, I pinned it to his gown as I wept like a baby. He never fully ascribed to the same faith as me, but he was also curious and hungry for whatever it was he thought I had. I knew he wouldn't mind, so I also prayed over him.

As the tears fell onto his hospital sheet, I suddenly heard the song "1999" by Prince begin playing over the hospital loudspeaker. What were the odds! I tracked down a nurse and asked her who controlled the music in the hospital. She said it was just the radio. It was just one of those moments in life where uncertainty and pain collide with gratitude and joy. The path had not been easy, but if it had been, I never would have met Tim. We would have never talked about life, faith, and everything in between. I never would have had such a poignant, sweet moment in that hospital beside his bed, a moment to honor his life and the way he treated people like me.

Tim passed away soon after.

New Problems and New Opportunities

We didn't have much time to process the grief of losing our friend and CEO because, as usual, we were thrust back in uncertainty. We all felt its weight. We had no idea what was going to happen to the studio. Eventually, Drew bought it from Tim's wife, and I ended up staying on for about another year and a half.

However, I felt a burning desire within to more intentionally pursue speaking and writing as a living. I spoke with Drew and we came up with a four-month plan to transition me out of the studio and roll over the accounts I was managing to someone else. Finally, I had a safe plan that would lead me to what I wanted to do!

Beware when the plan looks safe. Uncertainty has a way of striking when you least expect it, which is why it is healthier to learn to expect it and accept it with as much grace as possible. After a gentleman's handshake, we were two weeks into our four-month plan when the studio lost its biggest client. Revenue tanked. Suddenly, six others and I were laid off. Solid ground was back to shaky ground.

I came home to tell Ksenija, who was in her own season of uncertainty. Her father had been diagnosed with pancreatic cancer. Three months later, he was in hospice. I mustered up the strength and told her that I had been informed I was being laid off—I had two weeks left to work. I didn't know how she would take it. But I remember her looking at me with tears in her eyes—not only tears of fear but also of courage. "Well, we don't have much money in the bank, but I know you've been wanting to do this for the last 10 years. I believe in you." Now tears were streaming down both our faces. In her irresistible humorous way, she broke up our little cry fest. "Now get out of here and go sell some gigs!" We laughed and embraced.

Her father passed away two weeks later, the same week my job officially ended.

Because of our past experiences together in the uncertainty, we were both energized to keep moving forward to what was next, even if it was difficult and unpredictable. I had been thrown out of the boat, so it was time to start swimming in the only direction available: to pursue speaking and writing as my full-time career. And Ksenija became a full-time caregiver for her dad in his final weeks of his life.

Henry Kissinger said, "The absence of alternatives clears the mind marvelously."[7] Have you ever been there? Sometimes, being stuck between a rock and hard place helps you find a secret crevice you couldn't see from outside your conundrum. Being confined can actually make you feel liberated to fully pursue the only path available. It is when we are overwhelmed by every choice imaginable, which is what we think we want, that we often prove true the wisdom of Danish philosopher Søren Kierkegaard: "Anxiety is the dizziness of freedom."[8]

I felt the opposite of dizzy. I knew I was inching closer to the way I was made to be. Consider it a calling or whatever works in your context, but you'll recognize it for yourself when you begin doing the thing you feel most equipped to do in life. Sure enough, I quickly had three gigs booked with enough money guaranteed to get us through the end of the year. Plus, I was beginning to book up fast in the next year. Everything was coming up Ostach!

Oh yeah, did I mention that the next year was 2020? Cue the music of uncertainty, yet again. The pandemic hit and all of my events canceled. My dreams came crashing to a halt. It was a tough time, as it was for most people. Soon, I was collecting unemployment. I looked at my wife, ashamed and worried. "This was not the way this was supposed to go," I sighed.

But Ksenija? She smiled warmly and said, "Just trust."

"Trust? But don't you think I should get another job?"

"Maybe, but not just yet. You've burned the ships. Let's see what happens."

Uncertainty abounded. We had hit countless hurdles. All felt like it was lost, but we had not lost connection. So, I went against my feelings and chose presence.

Just then, at a pivotal moment in modern history that no one saw coming, a little company called Zoom burst onto the scene. Furthermore, as people around the world were faced with a physical and mental health crises like we had never seen in our lifetimes, my focus on connection and digital wellness became a critical need for organizations all over the world. My business blew up—in a good way! Over the next two years, I led more than 200 virtual events with organizations at a global level, entities I would have never had a way to pitch, much less reach before.

No one wanted the pandemic, but as has been the case throughout history, a moment of great uncertainty produced an opportunity to lean into the discomfort and let my presence abound in helping others. To be clear, your experience during the pandemic may have been much more tragic, perhaps even leading to the death of family or loved ones. I'm not saying that this horrible global tragedy was something I'm glad happened. I'm saying that all uncertain, difficult things produce opportunities for us to rise up in some way and be present, seeing the needs of others and meeting them in ways never thought of before.

But in the beginning of the story, I couldn't see the end. Neither can you. I had felt emotionally crippled from the weight of the uncertainty I was facing about the future. But these experiences equipped me to realize that most of life is day-by-day. It may sound trite or cliché, but it is true nonetheless. As my mentor used to say, "Thank God for our daily bread." This is a historical reference to the Israelites escaping from Egypt and being sustained for 40 years in the wilderness by special bread they picked up from the ground every morning to eat for the day. The only caveat was they couldn't store it up for the next day. They had to learn to trust, even amid the fear and uncertainty that perhaps the bread wouldn't be there tomorrow.

No matter the uncertainty you face, never give your presence away to satiate your fears. It won't work and tomorrow morning, there will be something on the ground you didn't know was coming. Your daily bread. If you're living, uncertainty comes with the territory. When we view it through a different lens, we see that uncertainty can actually be a gift.

Gift or Scarcity

It's hard to be uncomfortable, but it is a necessity for growth and presence in this world. Jon Acuff writes, "Feeling uncomfortable is just a sign that my old comfort zone is having a hard time keeping up with me."[9] Change only comes through discomfort, and each person's unique discomfort produces unique change. That's one of the reasons I believe everybody is a gift. Your gift is being developed and wrapped as we speak by the experiences you are walking through, and especially the ones riddled with uncertainty and difficulty.

Do you see yourself as a unique gift to those around you, or do you see your uniqueness as a problem? Or perhaps you don't see your uniqueness at all. These chapters have helped us learn to awaken to the inner gift, that is, to our presence and how it works and grows in the experiences of our lives, if we will let it. As we enter Part II, we will explore how to begin unwrapping and sharing this gift to those around us.

As we end this section, I hope you have pondered more deeply how you are uniquely created, that is, in your gifts, your abilities, your personality, and your life experiences. Whether a high school graduate about to head off to college or a high-level executive who feels lost between jobs after being laid off in the latest artificial intelligence boom, we all must keep exploring our own purpose for being here on this planet.[10]

The great news is that the purpose of your life is not about you. As my friend and fellow author Dave Wilson often says, "You are here to make a dent wherever you're sent." If you want to make the biggest dent, you need to understand how you're made and shaped. You must know yourself before you move forward in a life that is present and meaningful in its impact on others and the world. I don't mean you should know yourself because you are the answer to your own problems. No, I mean you should know yourself so you can humbly realize how to be present with others and allow them to be present with you—so you can invite something deeper and higher into your life than just your own perspectives and viewpoints.

Otherwise, it is all too easy to fall into a scarcity mindset in which not only is life always about you but it also features a gaping hole at the center of every thought and action you have—and nothing is ever sufficient to fill it. You can't be present for anyone else because you keep falling into the hole of your own negative mindset. Scarcity mindset kills presence. Pa Ingalls was grateful, despite his real scarcity, but it takes a certain set of practices to see what is good in your life as just as real as what is uncertain or difficult.

Which brings us full circle to the challenges of our modern, digital lives. The entire internet is designed to remind us of what we don't have. It spins us over and over again into the vicious cycle of chasing the appearance of fullness, even after we've learned the hard way that it always leaves us empty. **We desire full, but we are addicted to empty.**

To be clear, I haven't arrived. I still struggle with awakening to the gift of connection and presence in my own life. This is my third book, but the struggles have never fully gone away. However, I have learned that the struggles don't have to control my life.

For me, presence comes from a grateful perspective, the kind that is difficult to hold onto in the digital world. When you're always being sold something you didn't know you needed, you keep finding scarcity. When you're always being compared to someone who looks "better" than you, you keep finding scarcity. When you're always scrolling to the next reel, chasing an unspoken promise of finding true mental fulfillment, you keep finding scarcity.

I have learned that I become more aware of my presence when I practice gratitude, thanking God for my family, my friends, and every speaking gig I get! But the tension remains because, man, do I want more gigs! What if they don't come? What if it all comes crashing down tomorrow? Worry and scarcity rob me of the present moment's joy. Gratitude lets me experience the present moment's joy.

Wherever you are in life, I know you face uncertainty. Let me encourage you that if your life was your grandma's chocolate chip cookie recipe, uncertainty is not only a key ingredient, it is the chocolate chips! Don't numb out online in an attempt to avoid the uncertainty of your real life. No, jump in with others you trust and stir those ingredients because they're the sweetest parts of living a life of purpose and presence as you connect with your purpose for being here. And if you don't subscribe to the God model, just consider the natural gifts you have—and who knows, perhaps you can also get paid to use them!

But regardless, awakening to presence is worth the discomfort—and it will lead us to unwrap the gift of connection to be shared with others.

Reflection

When life feels uncertain or uncomfortable, do you tend to escape, control, or numb—or can you practice staying present long enough to listen to what the moment is asking of you?

A Poem

As we conclude part one, I want to leave you with a poem I delivered as a spoken word at a TED Talk several years ago. If we are awaken to presence and to enter into true connection with others, we must be willing to disconnect from that which steals our presence. That's what this poem is all about.

Every morning when I wake, my phone goes
straight up to my face,
Like makeup making me disgraced, it's still a thrill
I choose to chase.
All my time alone concealed, though it's loneliness
I always feel.
Belonging is the biggest deal, but online I can't be
that real.
Logging in means checking out to what this life is
all about,
Face-to-face where friendship sprouts, holding hands
and branching out.

So listen to these words I state and make them
yours and yours to break.
Say them with me. Say them proud. Grab your
phones out and sing out now.
Disconnect me! Oh, disconnect me! Take my phone
and shut it down!
I plead these words. I plead them now!

But up and down my eyes they go, scrolling on
from post to post.
These aimless updates make me choke, but still I
choose to hold this phone.
My buzzing friend, he makes me sick. He's in my
hand or he's on my hip.
He's growing and he's got a grip, like King Kong
pounding with his fists.
And urgency, emergencies, they're coming from my
daily feed,
My calendar, it cannot breathe, and my mind
collapses to its knees.

So listen to these words I state and make them
yours and yours to break.
Say them with me. Say them proud. Grab your
phones out and sing out now.
Disconnect me! Oh, disconnect me! Take my phone
and shut it down!
I plead these words. I plead them now!

PART II

The Shared Gift: Expressing Connection

Connection begins with vulnerable intentionality.

7 Unwrapping the Gift

"What lies behind us and what lies before us are tiny matters compared to what lies within us."

—Ralph Waldo Emerson

Now that we're learning what it means to begin awakening to our inner gift, we will explore how our inner gift can be shared with others—and why it can be so hard to do so in the modern digital age. Communication is more of an art than a science. It takes vulnerability, curiosity, and, ultimately, trust, to move from inner awareness to outer connection, whether in our personal lives, our business interactions, or in the way we relate to the world at large. Our inner gift is the part of us that can be authentically expressed in front of our friends, coworkers, or strangers on a plane—the place where we feel confident being comfortable as we are. But unwrapping and sharing the inner gift can be harder than we think.

Just ask my Grandma Teresa.

My dad's side of the family is Polish, while my mom's side is Irish. Each side brings its own richness of traditions. Well, some of the traditions didn't feel quite as rich. My grandmother on my father's side loved to procure matching pajamas for all fifteen grandchildren. With each passing year as I became older, the pajamas became less and less cool. The only consolation was that it was a shared embarrassment—my brother, sister, and all my cousins had to endure the uncoolness alongside me.

Eventually, the pajama tradition ran its course (thank God) and we transitioned to the white elephant gifts. This is where each person opens a gift in a certain numbered order, and each person has a certain number of "steals" when they can take anyone else's gift already opened. It was fun until it was not. That game is not for the faint of heart and there is always someone more cutthroat than the rest who ends up stealing a gift they probably shouldn't. Tears would often flow.

Sometimes, the kids cried, too.

But finally, we landed on my favorite tradition of all: the unwrapping challenge. This involved splitting the family into two teams who each have a box covered in many layers of wrapping paper. The goal is to peel off one of the layers and pass it to the next person on your team to see which team can unwrap the entire box first. But there is one little wrinkle: you have to wear oven mitts the entire time.

The first year we tried this new game, my grandmother was picked to go first for our team. Now Grandma was no slouch and had no shortage of capabilities. She became a widow at 50 when most of her children were still in their impressionable teen and young adult years. She raised them by herself with grit and grace.

She possessed a strong work ethic and an acute attention to detail. Even in her later years, I remember her sweeping the driveway, even when there was seemingly nothing on it to sweep. But she was also so fun! She'd chase us kids around, giving us a little smack on the "dupa dupa," as she would say it. (That's "backside" in most Slavic and Polish traditions.) She didn't sit to the side during our games, so we were all excited to watch her unwrap the first layer.

Maybe it was the lack of strength of her hands in old age, but when the game began, Grandma simply could not unwrap the first layer of that box. At first, we were all amused and laughed at the whole thing, but as the other team unwrapped all their layers to reach the 15 lottery tickets in the box, Grandma started to get actually frustrated. After all, she was used to working hard and accomplishing things. Finally, she threw the box down in frustration.

Unwrapping the gift of your own presence so you can be a gift of connection to others can also be frustrating. First of all, your unique inner wiring and personality already wraps the inner gift in many layers. It can be a struggle to peel them back and return to the core of who you are. But there is a great gift inside much more valuable than lottery tickets.

Also, there are your emotional oven mitts—things like insecurities, personality traits, and life experiences that tend to keep you more reserved. Even if you have somewhat awakened to the inner gift, sharing it with others can be difficult, but it is worth the work.

The Science of Being Stuck

These days, I find it helpful to explore how mental health, faith, modern technology, and our understanding of the human psyche all inform the process of unwrapping and sharing the inner gift with others. There is no shortage of pop psychologists, traditional psychologists, and therapists researching and writing about these exact issues. New breakthroughs in neuroscience and cognitive development continue to happen across the field of mental health. But for me, few are as groundbreaking and practical as internal family systems, or IFS.

I first learned about IFS from the keynote speaker who followed my speech at an event in Arizona for over 300 human resource professionals. I had long admired the work of Britt Frank from afar, so I was super excited to finally get to meet her. She is a licensed neuropsychotherapist and an expert on a unique topic of which one of her bestselling book titles says it all: *The Science of Stuck*.[1] Britt helps her patients and audiences break through inertia to find their path forward.

Britt's book is well researched and highly relevant, adding compelling insights into the process of listening to your inner self rather than avoiding it or fighting it, which often leaves us stuck. Between my opening keynote and her closing keynote at the conference, she and I had a wonderful conversation, even though it only lasted about 10 minutes. Our interaction was pleasant, but I could tell she had a deeper story and I was eager to hear it someday. Little did I know that someday would be that same day.

As she stood on the stage in front of a professional audience, within the first two minutes, she unwrapped and shared her inner gift by sharing her story. In her twenties, she had worked as a corporate executive at an advertising agency. Things seemed to be going well on the outside, but behind closed doors, she was hiding an addiction to methamphetamines. Suddenly, you could hear a pin drop. She continued to reveal that she was also stuck in an abusive marriage, as well as a cult-like church in which she had become completely immersed in a way that made her feel like she couldn't leave. I could not believe her level of vulnerability, or the fact that she was still alive and standing in front of us.

But eventually, Britt experienced a radical change that brought both sobriety and freedom from her addictions and unhealthy attachments. Yes, it took a lot of hard inner work and therapy to finally be able to move past that stage of her life, but she did it. She got unstuck. She spent the next 20 years of her life (and counting) dedicated to helping others in similar situations get unstuck as well. Her talk was inspiring and empowering, to say the least.

As soon as she left the stage, I approached her and asked if she would take a "walk and talk" meeting with me. Oftentimes, speakers at events find time to connect after they're done speaking because they have extra time waiting for their flight home or to the next event. There was an outdoor mall area surrounding the hotel's conference space, so she agreed to do a few laps with me. The talk went from me offering positive feedback on her keynote to a full-blown, 45-minute therapy session for yours truly about some of the places I was stuck.

This was when Britt introduced me to internal family systems. First developed in the 1990s by family therapist Richard Schwartz,[2] IFS is a therapeutic model based on the idea that none of us is only one thing inside, even though we tend to think of people as either bad or good. Nice or mean. Fun or boring. But IFS therapy is based on the concept that each of us have multiple distinct inner "parts" of our personality that function like members of a family, each with their own perspectives, emotions, and roles.

Just as we each have an external family in which different family members interact with one another, whether positively or negatively based on that particular person in that particular situation, we also have an internal family, parts of ourselves that have unique dynamics of interaction with one another differently in different situations. These are not multiple personalities. We already use parts language every time we say something like, "A part of me wants to eat Chinese tonight, but a part of me wants pizza." IFS is a parts-based modality to help us stop oversimplifying our inner messages and beliefs that lead to detrimental reactions and behaviors, the ones that keep you from unwrapping your inner gift and sharing it with others.

Instead of hating yourself every time you repeat a certain pattern, one you've been doing for years, the idea is to welcome (without shame) and befriend your inner parts. They often become activated and scared in certain circumstances, especially when they are facing repeated patterns that have hurt you before. Instead of reacting as loudly as that part within you is yelling or crying out in anger, fear, or anxiety, you can slow down and try to understand why it is reacting that way so your core self—the truest you—can offer it compassion and clarity and take back control of the health of your inner self.

A library of books has been written about IFS, and we are limited to how deep we can go into it in this chapter without skewing off topic. However, I find that just entertaining the idea that you are not only one thing is pretty liberating. When you are angry, anxious, or depressed, it's easy to feel like your whole self is just one big problem. But when you realize that there are different things going on inside you, you can at least begin trying to understand yourself rather than just judging or making excuses for yourself, whatever side of the coin usually suits you.

I encourage you to further explore IFS—once you're done reading this book, obviously. You might even start with one of Britt's books on the subject: *Align Your Mind: Tame Your Inner Critic and Make Peace with Your Shadow Using the Power of Parts Work.*[3] Now, back to my walk.

I learned two things from my short time with Britt. First, there are a lot of people in this world who are more stuck than they'd like to admit. Second, just like Grandma's oven mitts, most people aren't quite sure how to begin to peel back the years of pain, reactivity, and shame that layers their uniqueness, gifts, and their calling. Doing this inner work frees up space to listen to the inner voice inviting you to spend more time pursuing the people, places, and work that brings you to life.

The Voice and the Light

As you now know, my life as a speaker and writer affords me the humble privilege of meeting many incredible and innovative thought leaders who help millions of people. What they do affects many lives, including my own. You see, what we do matters, even if our influence doesn't reach millions. And the smallest of actions can sometimes make the biggest of differences.

One of my favorite authors—and human beings—is Parker J. Palmer. We've never met, but I've read just about everything he's ever written. At the time of this writing, he is in his mid-eighties. But back in 1999, he penned the book *Let Your Life Speak, Listening to the Voice of Your Vocation*. A 25th anniversary edition was released back in 2024.[4] Palmer marries the idea of vocation to one's calling because oftentimes, our career is a necessary means to an end. A career can merely be a job—an opportunity to earn money for our families. A vocation, however, is something we were made for and designed to do.

The careers we hold can easily suppress the calling we have, which leads to a lack of joy and satisfaction in our day-to-day living. After all, work takes up so much space in our lives, especially when we are middle-aged. Don't get me wrong—we must have careers. Everyone in the world is not entitled to get paid to do their passion; that is a modern generational misnomer. However, you can be fulfilled doing a job that isn't your dream job, but only if you also understand your vocational calling—that is, not just what you do at your job, but what you are made to do here on this earth.

Most people will never unwrap the gift of doing their dream job, but everyone is a gift themselves to be unwrapped and shared with this world. The key is knowing your vocation, regardless of your job. And knowing your vocation is really about knowing yourself. As Palmer writes, "We find our callings by claiming authentic selfhood, by being who we are . . . . The deepest vocational question is not 'What ought I to do with my life?' It is the more elemental and demanding 'Who am I? What is my nature?'"[5] I remember this distinction becoming apparent in my own journey as I spent years working creative jobs alongside amazing people, but deep down, each experience only served to enhance an ever-emerging desire to pursue my true vocation.

Knowing this elemental part of yourself is the first and indispensable part of awakening and amplifying your voice to the world. Palmer continues, "the word vocation itself . . . is rooted in the Latin for 'voice.' Vocation does not mean a goal that I pursue. It means a calling that I hear."[6] But when every space around you and within you is filled with the incessant noise of the digital age and its demands for your attention, hearing this calling can be difficult. There is so much that tries to drown out the most important voice inside.

Parker wrote this book before the digital age, but even he struggled to hear the inner calling to his unique vocation. He fought to kennel what Winston Churchill called the "black dog"—that is, depression.[7] It's easy to think of the widespread issue of depression as more of a modern problem, but even before smartphones and incessant scrolling, people have suffered from it for millennia. Iron-willed heroes like Churchill, who stood strong in the face of the greatest existential threat in the modern age, still had to deal with that pesky black dog inside.

Throughout history and even into the modern age, many people have felt compelled to mask their depression as if it were a secret scarlet letter of weakness and shame that should remain hidden. When we feel shame, we tend to silence our voice and avoid offering our gift to those around us, much less the world. Parker was right there. In his mid-thirties, he became so depressed that he couldn't even get out of bed. Then one day, a friend stopped by to see him. He didn't offer judgment. He didn't offer the perfect motivation. He didn't offer stellar advice. Instead, he chose being over doing. Presence over perfection. Calling over fixing. He offered just to be with him.

And that's what he did.

For weeks on end, Parker's friend sat with him. They didn't talk much. Rather, they simply listened to the birds outside. Parker says it was one of the most powerful experiences of his life that helped put the black dog back in his kennel, though for all of us, he barks and tries to dig his way out. Yet, Parker couldn't publicly talk about this experience until six or seven years afterward. It took that long to integrate these experiences into his sense of inner self.

But make no mistake: this was a key part of knowing himself, even though it wasn't easy to accept. Over time, he became more comfortable expressing how such places of inner darkness live alongside the places of light. Both are there and knowing both is essential to knowing the true self and cultivating health therein.

Darkness left unaddressed only gets darker. But darkness that is courageously acknowledged has the chance to be affected by light. **Darkness consciously held is less likely to bring us down than darkness subconsciously denied.** Britt's and Parker's experiences both demonstrate how being willing to acknowledge the darkness to a trusted source, even if only by the act of allowing someone to sit with you in it, can bring new and unexpected rays of light. Yes, there is always more work to be done in the way of therapy, recovery, and the like, but the reason all these are effective is they are based on the same principle: be honest with yourself as you are honest and present with someone else.

This principle helps you begin to remove the layers of darkness and stuckness wrapped around your gift within, unmuting the voice of your calling and freeing you to give it away to others with passion and purpose.

Deciphering the Inner Voice

All this talk of gifts, callings, and vocations sounds great, doesn't it? That's because such ideas and words awaken something inside of us. We all want our lives to count for something bigger than ourselves.

We all want to leave this world better than we found it. We all want to be who we were made to be in a way that unwraps to the world the unique gifts within us.

However, none of this talk should be taken to mean that only "big" things count when it comes to unwrapping our gifts. I'm not talking about fame, fortune, or notoriety. To be clear, if you set out to find these, you will most likely fly right over miles of real people with whom you were meant to walk, the hard way, over time. Being real with real people is the only true path to sharing the gift of yourself. As a friend of mine says, **"I used to want to be well-known; now I just want to be known well."** Obviously, there is no greater example of this than your family. Loving and serving them is the highest calling. If you make it big as a father or mother, you've made it big in life!

Even in business circles, the path to the kind of significance that makes a positive, lasting impact only goes through service toward others, and especially those in need. Yes, I know businesses exist to provide goods or services that can produce and sustain profitability, but in the end, ultimately, it is people who are affected, positively or negatively, by what they do. Without people, there would be no business. Companies that gift something greater to the world are those whose leaders never let the bottom line become the top rung of their ladder to success. They refuse to climb over a lot of people on their way up to something that will not leave a positive, enduring legacy.

Beloved philosopher and theologian Dallas Willard speaks to the relationship between calling and vocation as it affects the greater good. "This is why each vocation is considered a 'calling.' As individuals and leaders form or join organizations or societies, their objectives would not be directed toward self-seeking gain. Instead, these groups would be 'called' to 'higher' ends, such as service to their profession or their clients, customers, and neighbors, and not for personal prosperity alone. Those motivated by love at the public level will care for the public, because they care for (love) the people who make up the public."[8] In the end, our collective organizational pursuits are intended to be gifts of love to our communities, and to society as a whole.

But what about you? On a personal level, what are you to do with these ideas of unwrapping your gift so it can be shared with the world? It would be tempting to take these ideas and immediately get to work. You now know enough of my story to know that I have nothing against you hustling to inch closer to your heart's true vocation, but the path to your calling doesn't begin with busier, louder, more frenetic energy.

It begins with listening.

Of all the opinions about the digital world and social media, which we may agree or disagree with, none of us can deny that our digital existence has made us poorer listeners. Just scroll through a comment thread and pay attention to what is actually being said. Rarely are these sentiments in true line-by-line reaction to whatever has been posted. Rather, the comment section has become merely another soapbox from which people can say what *they* want to say. Did you catch that? We are now more prone to grandstand our own ideas than we are to give room for someone else's to truly be heard and considered. We already know what *we* want to say long before we've finished hearing what *they* want to say.

This listening problem isn't just *between* us—it's also *within* us. The path to hearing one's calling is a long and winding one, not for the faint of heart, but it is also not impossible for anyone to tread. But we must be more willing to listen than we're willing to speak or work for it. Speaking and working will eventually come, but they must follow the act of listening if we are to find our true vocation.

Palmer explores how the very act of listening for the voice of your vocation cultivates both joy and impact in your life's work. Let's be careful here. I'm not talking about a "me-first" culture that obsesses over one's own life, ignoring the lives and needs of others. No, I mean listening for the voice out of a desire to help and serve others with your own unique gifts.

Are your gifts truly unique? I believe they are. After all, your body is unique and unlike anyone else's. Even if you are an identical twin, you don't have identical fingerprints or DNA. To that end, there is such thing as a voice print—that is, your voice is literally the only one like it in all of history. Your voice print is literally as unique as you are and nobody has the same voice. Is it any wonder that finding your own voice is so key to finding your calling in life?

Always remember: hearing this unique inner voice is for the purpose of using your outer voice in your vocation in a way that betters the world. You can have an impact with the way that you're made. You can avoid pursuing activities, careers, and relationships that don't align with the inner voice. You can gratefully embrace a life that affects others, beginning with those inside the four walls of your own home. Finding your calling reframes your viewpoint of success and failure. As Author Bob Goff writes, "I used to be afraid of failing at something that really mattered to me, but now I'm more afraid of succeeding at things that don't matter."[9]

Hopefully, you're beginning to see how everything we discussed in Part I dovetails into our ability to connect with those around us—and to affect them in ways that matter. If our devices and digital practices rob us of presence, then we won't be able or willing to work through the challenges of peeling off the layers that hide and insulate our gifts from being known and experienced by those who need them the most. We'll keep getting frustrated like my grandma.

Or worse, we'll be like those in the modern age who, on witnessing someone being attacked or otherwise in distress, follow their first and modern instinct: pull out their phone and record rather than offer help. Hear me: the world needs the gift that you are, so it's worth unwrapping it—seeking to be unstuck—so you can first know it for yourself.

If you're not present, then you can't be a present to others.

Reflection

What parts of yourself have you been protecting, hiding, or withholding—and what would it look like to see them as a gift rather than a burden?

8

Delta Diaries: Finding Your Connection Zone

"Life is lived in moments of transition."

—Parker J. Palmer

"Whom did you meet on the airplane today?" When you travel as much as I do, you become accustomed to certain routines and rituals. This particular question is always one of the first things I hear from my wife when I get home. She knows that I always have a story. Since I usually fly on Delta Airlines, I've come to call these stories the *Delta diaries*.

But the Delta diaries are more than mere stories—they are insights for learning how to make room for real connection so you can share your inner gift more freely and effectively.

The interior of an airplane is a unique place to be. Can you imagine what our ancestors would think about sitting down in a metal tube with wings as you jet through the skies at 30,000 feet and more than 500 miles per hour? The experience has become normalized for us, but if you take off your modern lens, you will see that it is still quite spectacular.

But I find it spectacular for other key reasons as well. Sitting on an airplane is the perfect environment for all kinds of things. You are forced to stay in your seat, which is why the flight attendant points out 30 times on the hour that the pilot has turned on the seatbelt sign. This may make some feel boxed in, but it can also be a unique chance to be present with yourself and others. Yes, sometimes I do occasionally watch movies or take a nap. I may also do some writing on my next book because there's no downtime like plane downtime (I really try not to use the words *down* and *plane* in the same sentence, but you get the point). However, more often than not, the plane is an ideal environment to connect with the person next to me.

I call it the *connection zone*, and, as we will discover, it is a prime example of tactical ways to connect with others—ways rooted in social sciences, behavioral neuroscience, and psychology. These enable us to become better connectors as we share *who we are* with *whom we're with*. This process will also lead us to the same realization I have had over the years: connection isn't reserved for special occasions or for people with special abilities.

You are made to connect—you just have to find the connection zone.

Hello, Neighbor

On countless airplanes, I've sat next to a multiplicity of people from all backgrounds and walks of life. Once I sat next to a Muslim woman and we talked the entire flight about her faith in Islam and my faith in Christianity, learning from each other what beautiful work happens when you're willing to look at problems through an interfaith lens. We both maintained our beliefs, but both of our lives became richer having flown next to each other.

Then there was the Texan, Thom, who smelled like he just retired from working 60 years at a tobacco factory. He and his wife (Thelma) were in their mid-eighties and flying to see their great-grandchild. We talked the entire flight, and as it turns out, he had a love for airplanes, born from his days as an airplane mechanic, beginning with his work on single engine planes as a young man. His wife had worked at a Texas ammunition factory for 30 years. She wore a shirt that said, "If You See Me Running, Duck!" Their charming Southern drawl and heartfelt stories made me feel a true sense of connection to them, one I would have missed if we had not sat next to each other and had been willing to take out our headphones. Speaking of headphones, after Thom and I stopped talking, I put my headphones in and started watching a National Geographic series on the four seasons of nature. Halfway through the first part, I noticed that Thom was watching right along with me, though he couldn't hear a thing! The connection zone may seem hard to find these days, but on an airplane, it's all around you—we can even share screens!

One of my most memorable connections came on a flight from Detroit to Mississippi. I sat in 14C, which was the middle chair. The gentleman on the end of the row stood up and kindly let me sit down next to him. When we realized no one else was going to sit in our row, I moved to the window seat to give us some space.

As I added some room between us physically, I asked him his name. With a friendly smile, he told me it was John. He was in his early sixties; I was in my early forties at the time. He asked me what I did for a living and after I told him, he reminisced about the good old days of being an entrepreneur and having a young family at home. There was a twinkle in his eye.

We talked from takeoff in Detroit until touchdown in Mississippi. I came to believe that John was placed next to me for a reason. He shared a story from some 25 years earlier when he had three young boys at home: 10, 8, and 6 years old. He was working as a general contractor, building homes and remodeling kitchens and baths. But at that time, he had a very small crew led by himself and one other guy. They would hire extra help as needed. But one day, for the first time in his life, John's little outfit ran out of work. What's worse, by the Friday afternoon of the same week, his wife told him they were also almost out of food.

It was one of those moments in life we all hope to never face, but sadly, many across the world and here in America face food insecurity on a regular basis. No money. No food. And no clue what will happen next. Despite what we often think people who face this situation might look like, they often look like John and his family: hardworking folks who just catch a run of bad luck.

John didn't want his boys to face undue worry, but as his wife reminded him on that Friday, the boys would be expecting their Saturday tradition the next morning: pancakes and sausages from Dad. He knew he couldn't hide their crisis much longer.

That Friday night, John and his wife scraped together the last of the leftovers in the fridge and fed the kids before sending them to bed. As you can imagine, he didn't get much sleep that night. The red light of the digital clock reading 5:00 a.m. finally taunted him out of bed. He poured a cup of coffee and headed to the garage to hide out, waiting to face the inevitable difficulty of the morning when not only would there be no pancakes but also there would be no breakfast. He began pondering what he could do to rustle up some food that day.

Feelings began to bubble to the surface. Shock. Then shame. Then a small panic at his core, a sinking feeling way down deep that wasn't subsiding. He whispered a prayer of desperation, nothing formal or fancy. Just raw and desperate, if not a little angry over the whole situation. He had done his best and it wasn't enough. What was he going to do? It may not be over food or money, but have you ever been there in some area or circumstance in your life?

As these feelings swirled within him, John looked up and saw that his neighbor from across the street was walking his way with his own cup of coffee in hand. He must have noticed that John's garage door was up and the light was on. John was in no mood for chitchat, but he also didn't want to face his family inside the house. He had nowhere to run or hide.

He knew the neighbor, but they weren't exactly close. They had always shared greetings or a wave when they saw each other across the street, and they each had loaned or borrowed the occasional tool over the years. They weren't good friends, but they were certainly cordial.

"Good morning," the neighbor said in a positive tone.

John tried hard to muster a response that would hide his inner turmoil and maybe save a little face at the same time. "Mornin'."

"I'm real sorry to bother you so early, but I saw your light on and here's the thing: my wife and I area moving out this weekend." John tried to look interested, but it was hard. The neighbor continued, "It's been a pleasure being your neighbor the last 18 years. We've loved watching your family begin to grow and we wish you all the best."

"Well, we hate to see you go," John said in the most convincing tone he could find. "Best of luck!" John reached out and offered a half-hearted handshake and the neighbor started back toward his house. But as he reached the edge of John's driveway, he turned around said, "Oh, yeah, John—I forgot to mention one thing: there's a bunch of groceries in our fridge that are gonna spoil. We can't take them with us. By chance, would you guys want them?"

We were 30,000 feet in the air reliving a story from 25 years earlier, but John told it as if it happened yesterday. Tears began to roll down his cheeks as he told me how he woke up his boys and had them help him pack several blue coolers with food—and they were never the wiser to true dire place the family had been in. Those groceries lasted for the next two weeks and by then, John had landed more work and from that point forward, the business grew and they never faced anything like that again.

John's story affected me in multiple ways in terms of the value of sharing our gifts and making room for real connection. We all need neighbors, those with a sphere of location or life circumstance that intersects our own. A kind word or just common courtesy goes a long way to build rapport and trust over time. And also, when in doubt, share your excess with those in your neighborly circles. You may never know what they are facing on any given day.

His story also speaks to the power of the connection zone, being willing to just show up next to someone and see what happens next.

It may seem random to sit next to a stranger, but sharing connection is an intentional act that requires both tact and grace. Wherever you are today, in the air or on the ground in your normal day-to-day, I promise there is someone with whom you can share your gift. You just have to take out your headphones—or whatever stress, task, or distraction is keeping your head down—long enough to see them. Engagement begins with willingness, but if you are willing, you are already halfway to connection.

A few more thoughts on the idea of neighbor. Seattle-based organization Chamber of Connection identified six points of connection (more on this in an upcoming section).[1] The first point is "know a neighbor." This means that to maintain modern social and relational health, each of us needs at least one trusted neighbor we can rely on for help with the little things like borrowing sugar, letting out the dogs, or mail pickup, all the way to full-blown emergencies. This builds both safety and belonging. Unlike our neighborhoods of even 20 years ago, today's research is staggering: many today do not have an emergency contact or a neighbor they could rely on for anything, big or small.

A neighbor doesn't have to be someone who lives close to you. It can be the folks you see in school drop-off lines, in your community gathering spaces, or at your place of worship. To that end, one of the ways I've brought a neighborly vibe to audiences I speak to is to lead them in a game called "Hello, Neighbor." The idea is brilliant, mainly because I did not come up with it. I actually learned it from a trauma psychologist.

I have everyone stand in a large circle so they are all facing each other. Then, I share a statement that if people agree with, they reply to with the simple words, "Hello, neighbor!" For instance, if the statement is, "I prefer coffee over tea," some 80 out of a 100 people in a circle often reply, "Hello, neighbor!" It can be anything innocuous like preferring early morning to late night or discovering who prefers dogs over cats. But then, the game becomes more personal.

"Alcoholism runs in my family." "I suffer from seasonal depression." "I believe the Detroit Lions will win the Super Bowl one day."

You know, I hit real pain points.

But the idea is that such exercises immediately draw you out of a larger circle of people and help you find your neighbors who may share interests, economic backgrounds, needs, or even vices. It's a beautiful and simple way to visualize and encourage community in a circle—and to remind us that no matter how isolated and alone we may feel, there are people all around us who could serve as our neighbors—if we will only have the courage to connect.

Beyond such exercises, however, there are a few other tactical approaches to connection that are worthy of further exploration.

The Johari Window

Showing up is in itself an act of vulnerability. What if you are ignored? (Sometimes you will be.) What if the other person doesn't reciprocate? (Sometimes they won't.) What if connection with a particular person is harder than you thought it would be? (Sometimes it will be.)

Regardless of the outcome on the other side of potential connection, you have a side—this side—that is solely yours. You are 50% of every relationship and interaction you have. Renowned marriage counselor Gary Chapman, author of the bestselling book *The Five Love Languages*,[2] talks about the ways every marriage (and any relationship for that matter) has the ability, if not the tendency, to build a brick wall between it. Each passive-aggressive interaction. Each unfinished conversation. Each unresolved conflict—they're all single bricks. The higher the wall gets, the harder it is to connect in the relationship.

Gary recommends taking responsibility for the bricks that are yours in your wall, even if the other person is not taking responsibility (yet) for theirs. Even if your shortcomings or relationship hurts make up only 10% of the bricks of your collective relationship, focus on removing your bricks instead of trying only to convince your spouse to remove theirs. If you focus on your bricks, the wall itself loses its strength and light will begin to peak through the cracks of the wall.

Yes, what the other person does matters, and, yes, everyone should take responsibility for themselves. But functionally, you are only in control of your bricks, no matter how much you want to be in control of everyone else's, too. Such control is not only an illusion but also a distracting drain on the right kind of energy you are fully empowered to display. And the thing is, when you humbly and graciously begin to remove your own bricks, it almost always leads the other person to do the same.

You have agency. You have a choice. You have a gift to offer, even if it seems no one is asking for it. Yes, that gift may be rejected, but the vulnerable act of offering it is still worth the risk. Why? Because living open-handed toward connection with others, for their good, is the integrated path to embracing good for yourself. Again, you can create good cracks where the light can shine through.

Light needs a window to shine through into a dark room. The Johari window is a helpful concept to reveal how such openhandedness is a vulnerable place to live, but also the best place.

The Johari window was created by psychologists Joseph Luft and Harrington Ingham in 1955 as a framework for understanding and approaching self-awareness and interpersonal relationships.[3] The name *Johari* isn't a person but rather combines their first names: "Jo" plus "Harry." (Better than "hairy joe window," I suppose.)

The visualized model uses a four-paned window to sort information about a person based on two factors: what the *self* knows versus what it doesn't know, and what *others* know versus what they don't know. We can't talk about trust-based vulnerability as a key to sharing genuine connection with others outside of the four quadrants these categories produce.

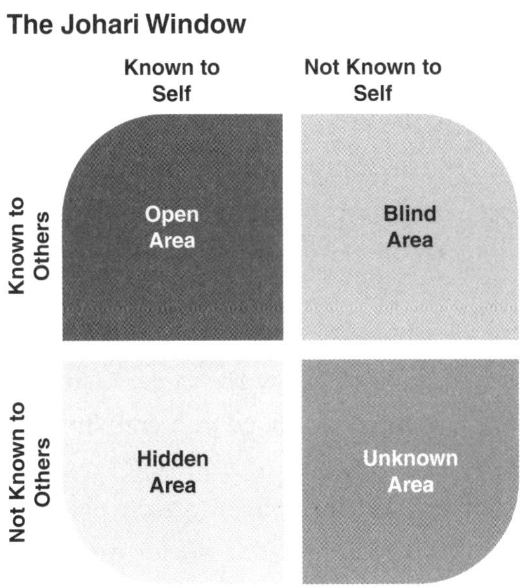

The first quadrant is called the *open area* (also sometimes known as the *arena*). As you can see, the cross-section of factors in the open area is that information about you is both known to self and known to the other person, or to others as a whole. So then, this is your most known self across the entire window. This quadrant describes those behaviors, attitudes, tendencies, and emotions that you're aware of and freely share with others. This is generally where you most want to be in connection as healthy relationships and effective teams tend to have a large open area.

The second quadrant is the *blind area* (or *blind spot*). In this area of the window, information is unknown to self, but known to others. We all have things that others can see about us but that we can't see about ourselves—habits, mannerisms, how others perceive your engagement, and the like. For example, maybe there are times when you think you are helping to fix a problem that is hurting your friend, but your friend feels you are being overbearing and judgmental. This is a quadrant we want to shrink, which can happen when we continue to move more toward self-awareness. Allowing trusted sources to identify and describe our blind spots can help a lot, which, again, can only happen when we lean into trust-based vulnerability.

The third pane is the *hidden area* (also known as *façade*). Information here is known to self, but unknown to others. These are the fears, insecurities, traumas, and leanings you choose to keep private and not share with others. We all have a hidden area, and many times in life, not telling everything is wise. However, while it is true that *everyone* in your life doesn't need to know *everything*, if you want your life to be characterized by being present in a truly shared, authentic connection, *someone* in your life needs to know *everything*. Can you see the difference? Many people think trust-based vulnerability means airing your dirty laundry to the world. Such an approach leaves "trust" out of the equation. But allowing yourself to be more deeply known to the most trusted of relationships through self-disclosure (some might call it confession) will lead you into new places of growth and connection.

Finally, the fourth quadrant is the *unknown area*. Here, information is unknown to self and unknown to others. This is the subconscious stuff like repressed memories, latent talents, or other things that have yet to rise to the surface. These are the emotions that in certain situations, seem to come out of nowhere. The thing is, though, nothing comes from nowhere. It comes from somewhere. From a connection standpoint, this quadrant may seem less important since these things are also unknown to others. However, that is not the case. The path to moving things out of the unknown area is best walked with someone else, that is, through conversation with trusted friends and family, therapy, recovery, contemplation, and other reflection-based endeavors. One cannot find their way through the unknown solely on their own.

Again, the Johari window is a tool to help you recognize patterns of thought, action, and connection so that ultimately you can continue to expand the open quadrant and shrink the blind area, hidden area, and unknown area, using the approaches and tactics just mentioned.

Though we will more directly address how the gift of connection affects larger organizational culture in the nonprofit space and the wider marketplace, it suffices to say here that the Johari window is useful for not only counseling and therapy scenarios for individuals and families but also for team building, leadership development, and communication training on the corporate level.

Regardless of how it is used, at the least the Johari window helps us stop oversimplifying the barriers to connection within ourselves and those around us. Much like the principle of parts in internal family systems discussed in Chapter 5 that says we tend to sum people up (including ourselves) as one thing, the Johari window expands our horizons to see that there is also more than one thing going on in the act of connection between people.

Within each of us, there are unknown areas, blind spots, and the like. Understanding these nuances enables us to approach ourselves and others with more grace, not expecting everyone to respond the same. We each bring different wiring and different stories to every potential moment of connection. Even so, if we are willing, we can always expand the open area as we lean into the gift of connection.

Six Points of Connection

The Seattle Chamber of Connection was founded by Aaron Hurst, launching a pilot location in Seattle in late 2024 into early 2025. My friend, Shasta Nelson, is the chief friendship officer at the Chamber of Connection and their team has a wonderful vision to expand nationally to combat what we've already described as a "loneliness epidemic." The six points of connection framework was created as a clear and actionable checklist for individuals and leaders to define and strengthen social bonds. To be clear, the organization didn't just make them up; rather, they drew on reliable research and pulled data from experts in the fields of psychology, healthcare, sociology, and urban planning[4]:

1. Know a neighbor
2. Find your people
3. Weekly social interactions
4. Third place
5. Close relationships
6. Civic engagement

We've already covered the first, but the other five are worth a gander as well.

The second point, *find your people*, encourages people to seek out groups with whom they share something in common. These can be cultural groups, alumni networks, faith communities, professional circles, parenting groups, or any other interest-based, life-season-based, or ideological-based commonalities. Yes, it is healthy to connect with strangers in general, but it is also true that a shared interest or experience builds comfort and trust among people who would not connect otherwise.

The truth is, the simplest principle of people-based connection is similarity itself. In his book *Influence*, social psychologist Robert Cialdini spent years studying "compliance professionals"—people like advertisers, salespeople, and fundraising professionals—to find what psychological triggers lead people to say yes. Again, while our context is not sales or marketing, the implications for connectivity are very valid.

One of the principles Cialdini identifies is the liking principle. It says we comply easier and more quickly with someone we like—and in general, we like people who are similar to us, compliment us, or cooperate with us. His research shows that perceived similarity—even superficial similarity—dramatically increases our willingness to help, trust, and give to others.[5]

One study he cites was set up to make people leaving a building think they were being asked randomly to give to a certain charitable cause. In truth, the researchers already secretly knew the people's names as the people thought they were there for a study inside the building, but the real experiment was in the parking lot when they came out. Intentionally, many of the people asking for a donation to a certain cause wore name tags with the same names as the people they were approaching. If the prospective donors perceived a shared a name with the people asking, their donations tripled! Why? Because on a subconscious level, they were more prone to like the person asking them for donations because of perceived similarities. Simple similarity produces more generosity of heart.

So why does all this matter? It matters because people have lost sight of how simple it is to connect—we just need to find basic commonalities and similarities to produce more trust and connection. It may be simple, but I acknowledge that doesn't necessarily make it easy. But what if more of us looked past our predilections to be either introverted or extroverted? What if we heeded even the simple ideas of connection found in shared reference points and perceived similarity? We would begin living as if these aren't just ways to strike up conversations for fun (though there's nothing wrong with having fun in conversations). We would see that people need us to stop looking past them and to engage. They need someone seeking commonalities, even if we may not look, dress, believe, worship, or cheer the same as them.

We don't have to be the same to connect, but even different people have more in common than they probably think. As the late British Parliament member Jo Cox said, "While we celebrate our diversity, what surprises me time and time again as I travel around the constituency is that we are far more united and have far more in common with each other than things that divide us." The unity is there for the taking—we just have to be intentional to never stop looking for opportunities to invite and engage.

Next is *weekly social interactions.* The idea is to try to experience at least two meaningful social interactions outside of home and work each week. Research shows it takes about six meaningful interactions to form a real friendship. That being said, it takes more than 200 hours to develop a close bond. Can you see how our devices keep us from the kind of social interactions that would keep from our feelings of loneliness and isolation? These things take substantial time, but if we ditch the devices and opt for human connection, we'll find that we actually have more than we think.

The fourth point is, well, *third place.* The term originated from sociologist Ray Oldenburg in his 1989 book, *The Great Good Place.*[6] Oldenburg's concept is simple: the first place is your home or the place where you live. The second place is your work, or where you spend your productive or earning hours. The third place, then, comprises those informal public gathering spots where community happens. Oldenburg contended that these third places—pubs, cafés, barbershops, bookstores, parks, diners, churches, and so on—are essential to civic life, democracy, and social well-being. They foster a sort of neutral ground where usually divergent groups of people can mingle. In these places, conversation is the main activity, and over time, regulars develop a sense of belonging. To Oldenburg, the decline of the third place has been a devastating loss to community connection and cohesion.

The penultimate takeaway in the points of connection is *close relationships*. This may seem redundant or counterintuitive at first, like telling someone that the easiest way to lose weight is to lose weight. Isn't the development of close relationships the whole objective of the six points of connection in the first place? The real point here is that we shouldn't let interest-based or location-based connections eclipse our need to continue pursuing positive, consistent, and vulnerable relationships. There's a reason someone can feel so alone in a large crowd—without true connection, there may be people present, but no present people. Develop all levels of connection, but don't settle for them when the close relationships sometimes prove harder to sustain. Keep trying. Keep seeking to identify people who make you feel a sense of belonging, then keep intentionally investing in those connections.

Finally, there's *civic engagement*. This one is pretty self-explanatory. Find a way to participate and volunteer in activities that better the community around you and enrich the lives of people on a larger scale than just your local neighborhood. This could mean running for office, but it more likely means showing up for a city council meeting, participating in a food drive, or joining a volunteer group to pick up trash on the side of the road.

Sharing connection with others is critical to their inner health, as well as our own. But remember, each layer of connection that we establish is not the goal unto itself, any more than getting a table at a restaurant checks the box of eating a meal. When we sit down, we have to actually order food and consume it. The same rings true for connection. Once we have the opportunity to be near each other, we have to actually engage in ways that build meaningful bonds of relationship, regardless of their level of depth. We cannot and should not connect deeply with just anyone, but still, we can connect meaningfully in some way with most everyone with whom we come into contact.

To end this chapter, let's explore one particular way we can make our momentary opportunities to connect meaningful.

Generative Dialogue

I understand that jumping straight into deep conversation isn't for everyone. We are not meant to become best friends with every stranger we meet on the street or on a plane. But in today's society, we've allowed the new rules of relational engagement established by social media and digital interaction to lull us into sleepwalking through our in-person connections with people we don't know.

We're so full of empty digital calories that we have lost our appetite to be curious and empathetic to the physical people around us. When we're all looking down, we don't notice each other. We're too busy living in an alternate world where connection is defined by image, emotion, and quantifiable likes—to the point that we don't really like the idea of putting forth the effort to talk to the people around us. Our energy is already depleted. It's no wonder then that so are our connections.

There are many downsides to such ways of thinking and being, the worst being that so many people carry their heavy mental weights alone. No one ever gets close enough to know the weights even exist. But my time on airplanes is just one of many examples of the beauty that surfaces when you generate dialogue with a stranger that lifts them up, provides them hope for the future, or simply enables them to get something off their chest. Such experiences led me to deploy what Jamie Winship, author and consultant, calls *generative dialogue*. The term was originally coined by organizational and learning expert William Isaacs as stage 4 (the highest stage) in his four-stage evolutionary model of dialogue. Isaacs developed this framework through the MIT Dialogue Project in the 1990s, building on the late American scientist David Bohm's earlier work on dialogue.[7]

Generative dialogue is the opposite of shallow dialogue. Shallow dialogue is talking about the news, the weather, or what you saw in your social media feed the night before. Such conversations may have a place at times, but when they become the norm instead of one component of communication, most of our conversations tend to yield little to no redeemable or even positive energy. In fact, shallow interactions generally deplete our energy, leaving us more tired when we walk away.

Generative dialogue, however, produces energy-latent interactions. It is the act of being intentional in conversation by asking questions that naturally generate the freedom to speak more specifically about what it is someone is truly feeling, sensing, or experiencing. Here's an example. Instead of asking someone "How are you doing?" you could ask them "What they are feeling excited about?" I include more generative questions in the back of the book for those looking to move beyond the dreary pitfalls of shallow dialogue (see the Appendix for more about generative questions).

For me, there are three key questions that best create generative dialogue, though I'm sure others could do the same. First, instead of the common question "What do you do for work?" I ask, "How do you spend your time?" The first question is usually shallowly interpreted. The second is not only broader and invites more information but it also creates room for the responder to ponder and share not only what they are required to do to survive but also what they value and enjoy, as evidenced by how they spend their time.

The other two generative dialogue questions I have found to be most effective are "What are you most proud of in the last 30 days?" and "What are you looking forward to in the next 30 days?" These questions not only invite specificity, which helps us swim past the shallows in conversation, but they also reveal a genuine interest in what the other person holds dear. When someone can reflect on what has made them feel good in recent days, or what they are currently feeling hopeful about, you'll be shocked by the difference in the quality of the conversation. You have opened the door for something better than they expected, even if they seemed annoyed or reticent at first.

I once shared a newsletter inviting families to use generative dialogue at their Thanksgiving dinner tables to avoid the awkwardness that often comes when family gatherings tend to produce either shallow dialogue or disruptive dialogue arising from historical family dynamics. One of my clients sent me a text with a picture of a large white sheet of paper on which a quadrant of four questions had been drawn. There was space for each family member to write down responses to these four generative questions: what are you proud of? What are you excited for? Who is someone you grew closer to this year? What is a lesson you don't want to repeat for next year?

She was surprised to watch everyone participate, from the teens to the parents to the grandparents. They read all of the answers aloud and it created a special moment for her family, all because she was intentional with the time and used it to generate new insights about each other.

The energy produced from generative dialogue is contagious. When these kinds of conversations are occurring, a certain vibe fills the air and everyone can feel it. Before you know it, people who didn't know each other 10 minutes ago will be doing all they can to maintain this energy. To me, it's like giving fresh water to someone who has only been given sugary drinks. They will always think they prefer the sweet taste and colorful label of a soda to a boring glass of iced water. But when someone is truly parched and they begin to take a few sips of cold, pure water, they will suddenly begin guzzling it down as fast as possible. Their bodies crave it, though their minds may not. The same rings true for generative dialogue—our inner selves crave what our digital selves reject.

On another flight from Raleigh, North Carolina, to Detroit, I sat next to an African American man about my age. His carry-on items made it obvious he was very tech-centric. He was a content creator with high-end camera gear and Ray-Ban Meta glasses that could record our entire conversation simply with the click of a button. We started off as strangers, but by the end of our flight, I was trying on his Ray-Bans and recording our conversation.

How did we go so far so fast? Did I just dive deep into places I was not invited? No, I literally asked him my go-to generative dialogue questions. When I asked him what he was most proud of in the last 30 days, he shared that he was proudest of his recent journey through therapy that had led him to become cordial with his ex-wife so they could be better co-parents together. Of course, this led him to unpack more of the therapy process and how he was beginning to become aware of the blind spots and shortcomings that had contributed to the distance that divided his marriage. As we know from the Johari window, our blind spots generally are not revealed until we have the courage to seek feedback from others. He was experiencing the growth of his open area and sharing the process served to energize him even more.

Before we knew it, he was also reflecting on the fact that he almost died in a car crash two years earlier, which happened directly after his divorce. At his lowest place both physically and emotionally, he began a journey toward healing. It was beautiful and we were both in tears as he unwrapped more and more layers. I didn't ask him for his whole life story, but I did my very best to listen to him with my ears, my eyes, and my body language. He didn't ask for my life story either, but when I shared, it was like the generative dialogue had already spread to him—he engaged with me the same way I engaged with him. By the time we landed in Detroit, we had both shared a mutual connection that enriched our lives.

Again, no matter who it is, from John to the Muslim woman to the Texan to the content creator, there were only two things they had in common: they were sitting next to me on the flight and one of us initiated generative dialogue out of a desire to connect. Some of them seemed low-key annoyed when I first started to engage, but none of them rejected my generative dialogue after the first question.

Again, people desperately need this type of interaction in the connection zone, even if they don't realize it in the moment. In the end, like them—and like you—what I instinctively want the most is for someone to really know me.

And by the way, if you ever see me on a flight and you put your headphones in, I'm still going to say hi!

Reflection

Looking back, where have you experienced the greatest sense of connection—and what patterns begin to emerge as you name those moments?

9

If You Really Knew Me . . .

"When we allow ourselves to be seen, we invite others to do the same."

—Brené Brown

The Delta diaries never fail to deliver interesting stories and even more interesting insights about being present and sharing connection with others. Over the dozens of flights I take each year, I've come to notice some patterns of how people travel. Specifically, when a plane lands and everyone's phones reconnect to their cellular service, approximately 70% of the passengers immediately text their loved ones that they have landed safely. How do I know what everyone is texting? I've asked many of them, just as a part of my research. Yet I do the same thing, always texting Ksenija with either a heart, a plane, or the prayer hands emoji.

Once as I contemplated this phenomenon on a small flight from Detroit to North Dakota, I decided to do a little more research by connecting with the two pilots and getting their take on it. I broke the ice by asking them if they would pose with me for a selfie. One of the pilots was of the baby boomer generation, probably in his late fifties or early sixties. The other was a millennial, probably in his early to mid-thirties. They answered my request at exactly the same time, talking over one another. The boomer said, "No," while the millennial said, "Yes."

Awkward.

It was one of the many moments out on the road when I wished I had my kids with me. No one could refuse posing for a selfie with those two cuties. Regardless, I had already asked, so I stood with the millennial pilot and snapped the photo before moving on to get off the plane and on to hotel.

I was new to North Dakota and I discovered that if you land late and take your time getting off the plane, you can easily be the last human standing in the airport—or perhaps in the entire state. It was a ghost town. On my Lyft and Uber apps, no drivers showed up as available. The car rental counters were also closed. The only way to get to my hotel was to wait for the hotel shuttle.

After about 20 minutes standing on a sidewalk in the middle of nowhere, the hotel van finally pulled up. I loaded my luggage and took my seat, eager to get to my room and find some sleep. It was well past midnight at this point. I was the only person on the shuttle, but the driver never put the van in drive.

"Hey, ma'am," I said gently, "any chance we could go ahead and leave for the hotel? I'm pretty tired."

"We will soon," she kindly replied, "but we're still waiting on a few more people."

A few more people? I was pretty sure that the driver and myself were the only humans in a five-mile radius, if not the universe, by this point. Suddenly, the airport doors opened and guess who climbed aboard the shuttle next to me? It was the entire flight crew from the plane, including the boomer pilot who obviously thought of me as a nuisance.

I was exhausted, yet I knew this was a chance to at least further my research, if not make some connections. I spoke up and asked the two pilots and the three flight attendants their guesses about the percentage of people who text someone that they have landed safely as soon as a plane touches down. Immediately, the flight attendants guessed 60%, 70%, and 80%. The millennial pilot spoke up next, chiming in with 85%.

The older pilot finally spoke up. "You know, I don't really care about that. I just want to make sure we've actually landed the plane and that people are safe. As long as that happens, I don't care about texting anybody." We all chuckled—not at him, but at the differences in priorities for various generations. I thanked them all for their opinions and eventually found my way to a hotel bed to get some much-needed sleep.

But as I lay in bed, I couldn't stop thinking about the flight crew and their responses—and specifically, the older pilot. First of all, I was fascinated by the shared behavior of most people in the digital age. There was a day not so long ago when, after a flight touched down, you had to at least wait until you got to the hotel or until you found a payphone to check in with loved ones. But now that we all can check in instantaneously, doing so is the expected norm. Less than two decades ago, no one expected to hear from you immediately when you landed. But now, if they don't hear from you as soon as the jet's wheels have touched down, it is cause for concern, if not panic.

To me, this speaks both to our need for connection and the ways modern technology informs the way we try to meet that need. It is another great example of the digital pulse becoming more recognizable as a sign of life than our actual pulse. Your loved one is probably fine if you don't hear from them, but since our connection is now based on the social parameters with smartphones as the hub of all connection, all of us are considered to be in danger until proven otherwise—and the proof of life comes through the phone. If it doesn't ring or ding, presence turns into panic.

But beyond this, the older pilot taught me that there is usually more going on inside someone than their initial reaction betrays. We can often reject someone's expression or opinion because it doesn't align in delivery with the way we would communicate. But in the case of the pilot, he wasn't anti-selfie; rather, he didn't get the point of it. In his mind, shouldn't his energy be expended actually landing the plane rather than texting about the fact the plane has landed?

At first, I thought the guy was kind of a jerk. But once I knew a little more about what made him tick, I found that he wanted the same thing the rest of us wanted: to get there safely. The world has always been divided, but technology has made us more aware of it than any generation before. This can push us to quickly sum people up by shallow interactions. It makes dismissiveness all too easy—after all, if you have your phone, you no longer have to even worry about talking to that jerk ever again.

But if you really knew him, things would feel different.

If You Really Knew Me

Generative dialogue is an effective tool for fostering more meaningful conversations and connections, but it is not the only way. Another tactical approach I often use with groups when I'm speaking is an exercise called *if you really knew me*. It is like a game that uses a common, simple prompt to help people get past the shallows of assumptions and stereotypes, because the quicker we can become more vulnerable and honest, the better chance we have to establish rapport, transparency, and ultimately, authenticity.

Vulnerability is a superpower when it's authentic.

A quick warning here. Using this exercise in the wrong situation or with the wrong attitude could make people feel like you're forcing vulnerability. Obviously, that is not the intent. Forcing connection is toxic to both individual conversations and larger group cultures. But if done correctly in an emotionally safe environment, encouraging vulnerability can remove a lot of the roadblocks to connection—especially among a culturally or generationally diverse or divided group.

It can happen around a table or sitting in a circle. Each person is invited to say, "If you really knew me," followed by something about themselves that goes beyond the surface level. Yes, you can warm up with lighthearted or funny facts, but as you warm up, people are encouraged to share something real, though obviously appropriate to the setting.

For example, if you really knew me, you would know I have a younger brother with special needs. And if you really knew me, you would know that I love to play piano, yet I haven't played as much since becoming an adult—and that I want to get back into it. If you really knew me, you'd know that my dad is battling mental and physical health issues, which can make it difficult for me to create the right boundaries to love and respect him while also continuing to mature as a man myself. If you really knew me, you'd know that I use Spotify playlists to help manage my mood. I've got playlists for writing, playlists for exercise, and playlists for most anything else you can fathom. You'd also know that I listen to Kenny G, the saxophone legend, when I want to feel close to fond memories of my dad.

As you can see, this exercise can quickly cover the gamut of real and fun. As people continue to go around the circle and share more things about themselves, they seem to become more and more empowered by realizing that they have more in common with the people around them than the college they attended, their zip code, or even their take on politics and religion. (I'd suggest avoiding those last two topics as much as possible.)

I have facilitated *if you really knew me* exercises all across the country, and they are always powerful. It also has a way of helping leaders connect with team members, closing the leadership gap through shared experiences and issues. C-suite leaders often feel the pressure of being transactional supervisors, always under the gun to grow their business and increase profits. They can let their shared humanity become eclipsed by a shared goal for growth or profit—and when the leader forgets their humanity, it is easy for the organization to develop a culture that doesn't value people and their stories. But when a CEO says, "If you really knew me, you'd know that I also struggle with anxiety," then the mid-level manager who just shared the same thing realizes, maybe for the first time, that her boss shares the commonality of humanity's pain.

To me, the best superhero movies are the modern ones that bring in an ensemble of superheroes instead of just one. If vulnerability is a superpower, shouldn't we want more than one of us to use it? Just think of the implications. If everyone in a family, religious organization, or corporation comes to an agreement about the importance of vulnerability as a feature and not just a bug, can you imagine what they could accomplish? And by "accomplish," I don't really mean the bottom line, though I think that will be affected, too. I mean that a culture of mutual trust and connection could become a shared value to be pursued on a regular basis.

Whether it's the *if you really knew me* exercise or any other attempt to connect, when we maintain rigid expectations about the outcome of the experience, we will almost always miss the forest for the trees. We have to remain flexible to ever-changing circumstances, reminding ourselves yet again that even though there is certainly a social science to social connection, it is as much art as anything else in terms of actual interaction with real people. We have to stay creative. We have to remain curious.

Curiosity creates opportunities to see things from someone else's point of view. And in her book *The Let Them Theory*, Mel Robbins writes about the various frames of reference each of us has. Fruitful communication occurs when we release the need to control others' actions or opinions, choosing to only take responsibility for our own responses and choices. In a digital world defined by images and opinions of self, we can easily forget that people's reactions come from their own experiences, fears, and worldviews. Usually, how they are reacting is more about them than it is about you.

In my case, it was my own frame of reference that was a barrier to possible connection. I felt like I didn't belong and that I needed to be ready to be someone I was not in order to connect. But when I could let go of that defensive stance and listen quietly and with curiosity, I experienced both inner peace and greater outer connection with those around me. I was able to stop worrying about who I am and instead let them be who they are.

That is the essence of seeking opportunities for connection. We have to be flexible and curious as we release assumptions or defensive postures. Connection is a two-way street, but if we're the ones trying to initiate it, we must remember that we're driving onto someone else's street. The neighborhoods may look different. There may be more speed bumps or different speed limits. In other words, we shouldn't expect connection with someone else to be identical to our own ways of connecting. We have to meet them where they are.

Connection opportunities are all around us, if we are willing to seek them out and follow through with vulnerability and curiosity. When we really know each other, we can't help but connect more naturally. Why? Vulnerability and curiosity are the very superpowers that bend the steel bars of isolation we've come to know and expect in our modern world.

Above Sea Level

I have had the honor of delivering two TED Talks, but anyone who watches these events on any level will remember Brené Brown's "The Power of Vulnerability"[1] delivered at TEDxHouston in June 2010. With more than 100 million views, it remains one the most widely viewed TED Talks in history.

I don't know anyone in the spaces of pop psychology or mental health who would say they haven't been inspired in some way by Brené's writing and speaking, even if they disagree on any singular point. She has achieved nothing less than celebrity status in these circles of influence, writing numerous bestselling books and becoming a household name in podcasting. She is known for being not only intelligent in the traditional sense but also emotionally intelligent. She helps people become brave as they dare to lead themselves, their families, and their organizations.

This is quite the impressive collection of accolades, yes? Sure it is, but it is all too easy to elevate someone so high that they become unreachable. The truth is, Brené is just like everyone else she interviews on her podcast or features in her books. She experiences nervousness, excitement, sadness, and sometimes, darkness and depression. In fact, she herself would never want anyone out there to think that there's such a thing as a superhuman who never experiences such things.

We're all broken—and though that sounds like bad news, it also means that we can empathize and support each other as we walk through common struggles and pains. We can step into dark together through mutual encouragement—that is, literally infusing one another with courage. As Brené famously wrote in her book aptly named *The Gifts of Imperfection*, "Only when we are brave enough to explore the darkness will we discover the infinite power of our light."[2]

Brené herself had a somewhat auspicious start to her public-facing career. One story in particular is a moment I have lived vicariously through for years, mainly because it's such a relatable experience and because it is funny enough to remind me to never stop laughing at myself.

Before all the acclaim, Brené Brown did what she continues to do today. For nearly a quarter of a century, she has been a research professor in the Graduate College of Social Work at the University of Houston. Her real breakout moment came when she delivered the aforementioned TED Talk of a lifetime. But there is always a backstory—and in this case, it is a backstage story.

As Brené waited to take the stage, she was riddled with nervousness. Who was she to speak to all these people? She was just a professor—who would want to hear what she had to say? Soon, the preceding speaker, an Australian man, finished his talk and came backstage to the sound of a rousing applause from the folks in the audience.

When Brené saw him, she said, "Wonderful job, mate!"

"Thank you," he replied with a slight chuckle, "You're going to do great as well!"

"I'm so nervous," she replied with an anxious shudder. "I can't believe how many people in suits are out there. I usually just speak to students and professors."

"Well, ma'am," he replied, "you're about to speak to a bunch of C-level executives."

Brené looked back at him curiously. "Yeah, that's what they told me."

The man picked up on her confusion and continued, "You know, they are C-level as in CEOs, CFOs, and so forth and so on."

Suddenly, Brené began to laugh uncontrollably. The man was befuddled as she tried to catch her breath. "*C*-level!" she huffed. "All this time, I thought they were telling me that this crowd is just down-to-earth kinds of people—you know, not-above-sea-level kind of people." Now they both laughed hysterically.

Brené could have saved face and kept her "sea level" mistake to herself. The guy never would have been the wiser. But instead, she chose vulnerability. She talked about her own imperfection as if it wasn't something to be ashamed of. In this case, she was even able to laugh at herself, one of the best kinds of vulnerability there is. Their conversation also had the effect of calming her nerves and enabling her to access her most authentic self before stepping onto the stage.

The rest, as they say, is history. As mentioned, she delivered one of the most widely viewed TED Talks of all time, and it all began with her willingness to share the gift of vulnerability. And in fact, her work inspired my first book entitled *Courage to Connect*, which I self-published in 2020. Can you see how the same energy that makes generative dialogue contagious also does the same when we are willing to be vulnerable with others?

I called my first book *Courage to Connect* partly because I was inspired by etymology of word *courage* itself. The word originates from the Latin *cor,* which means "heart." This is why Brené redefines courage as, "to speak one's mind by telling all one's heart."[3] It is not about heroic acts as much as it is about heroic presence. Through this lens, when we say someone has courage, we're saying they share their heart or tell their story with the kind of openness that evokes a sense of trust or conviction. Like a heartbeat, such courage is evidence of life, but also of a real, messy life being lived with others and not in protective isolation.

Real courage is learning to speak the dialect of the heart.

Yes, I realize that this comes more easily to some than to others. I am a natural empath who, as I said before, seems to be fluent in all five love languages (which is not generally a thing). I am also an Enneagram Type 2,[4] which is the helper. I instinctively feel the needs of those around me and move to meet them, sometimes to the detriment of my own health and well-being. So, yes, these things naturally enable me to draw closer to people, but everyone is not wired that way. We all come from different backgrounds, upbringings, and dispositions. Even in the workplace, some companies have four different generations under one roof, each of them with different levels of comfort on how they share or connect, not that connection styles are purely generational in nature.

The point is, we don't all have to be Brené Brown or deliver TED Talks. Right there in your cubicle, in your car, in your living room, at the ballfield with your kid—wherever you are, you can learn to live courageously through your connections with others, making it less necessary for you to ever say, "If you really knew me . . . ."

Because people who spend any time with you at all really would know you.

Sharing Is Caring

"Sharing is caring" is a common expression that, for the most part, only surfaces in early educational environments. The odds of seeing or hearing these words in a kindergarten classroom are astronomically higher than seeing or hearing them in corporate office. At some point, this sentiment begins to sound too childish to adults, or perhaps something we file away in a mental folder labeled *already fully learned*. But I think our unconscious dismissiveness of the simple sentiment behind this seemingly elementary expression may be the reason kindergartners connect more easily with each other than today's average adults.

I know it would be easy to say, "Yeah, but a little kid's world is so much simpler than mine. I mean, what do they really have to talk about beyond playgrounds, paste, or Play-Doh?" It's a fair point in the sense that kids cannot access the same depth of conversation as adults. However, what we miss here is that connection is not only a matter of depth of content. It is also a matter of shared experiences, shared emotions, and, ultimately, an open-handed shared humanity. Even if we're not bearing all the details of our souls and stories, we can still deeply connect when we share the human experience together with empathy and without judgment.

In other words, eating the same Play-Doh can do us all some good. (This is not medical advice.)

The other real issue with an adult application of the idea that "sharing is caring" is that when we first adopted this idea as kids, the implications were much more concrete than abstract. For the most part, we were being encouraged to share a literal toy with another kid who wanted to play with it. We weren't exactly sharing details of our human experience—we just wanted our turn on the Etch-a-Sketch. But what if we clear the cue on this concept and reapproach it in our collective adulthood—that is, shake the Etch-a-Sketch and start all over? We will discover that the "sharing is caring" concept is true and effective in both a concrete and an abstract sense.

In the concrete sense, as adults we still need to share material possessions and monetary support with those who have need, as much as we are in the financial position to do so. Meeting each other's needs is a key to human connection. When you share what you have with someone who is struggling to have enough, you quite literally express the fact that you care about them in a tangible way.

To be clear, this isn't merely about the wealthy giving to the poor. The concepts of wealth and poverty are pretty polarizing in today's world, often used to rage-bait one side or the other into angrily or heartlessly pursuing whatever political course certain bad actors manipulate us into. It is not a political statement to say that we're being divided from each other on every front imaginable, including the wealth gap. It is merely a fact of the digital age and the effective mobilization that social media promises and provides.

The sharing of physical needs process I'm referring to is about mutual respect, empathy, and concern, humbly realizing that each of us has been blessed in some way for the higher privilege of blessing others. We're not intended to selfishly hoard our singular opportunities and unique gifts as we angrily judge others for the way we conclude (with little evidence beyond a social media–informed viewpoint) that they have squandered their own opportunities and gifts. What a waste of both energy and resources, and what a shame to be rich, yet still so angry that our riches change no one's lives but our own.

Sharing is caring because giving is living. When we give the gift of connection in tangible ways, we actually lift the fog of our own anxiousness and feel alive in ways we never thought possible.

It is such a profound process, and yet your kindergarten teacher knew it the whole time.

Well done, Miss Weber. Well done. (Also, can I have snack time?)

That's the concrete approach to "sharing is caring." The abstract approach—the one we've been missing—is just as revolutionary and integral to healthy connection. The application is more in the vein of what we've been already been discussing re-approach: sharing our stories, vulnerabilities, and experiences without fear and judgment. The sequence is life-giving, yet so simple. When we share, we can relate. When we relate, we can belong. When we belong, we experience the sense of wholeness and unity the entire world longs for in this divided digital age. This makes it super important how to show up in the digital world toward others.

"To post or not to post" is starting to feel like the modern creator's Hamlet moment—not because posting is difficult, but because the audience is changing. Our social feeds are filled with bot-generated content, recycled AI summaries, and engagement that *looks* human but isn't. As a growing share of online impressions come from nonhumans, it's fair to ask what we're actually buying with our time. Imperva's "2025 Bad Bot Report" found that automated traffic surpassed human activity in 2024, accounting for roughly 51% of all web traffic, with so-called bad bots responsible for 37%.[5] While not limited to social media, these findings betray a broader truth: the internet has become an ecosystem where machines talk to machines, and humans are often bystanders.

This isn't just annoying. This is shaping our lives together. Researchers at Oxford's Computational Propaganda Project have documented how bots and automation manipulate online discourse, particularly in political contexts, turning platforms into environments where amplification can be fabricated rather than earned through trust.[6] Studies from Carnegie Mellon suggest bots can account for a significant share of online participants—about 20% in some analyses—meaning online engagement is no longer a reliable reflection of online connection with real people.[7] Stanford's Internet Observatory has further shown how inauthentic accounts and artificial intelligence

(AI)–enabled spam networks manufacture credibility and scale, blurring the line between what is real and what is performed.[8] The question, then, isn't simply *Should I post?* but *What kind of posting can create real trust, real community, real outcomes rather than merely feeding the machine?*

Our digital pulse urges us to post, while our physical and emotional pulse quietly suffer the consequences. Even as content production increases, its human impact continues to be diluted. Fewer real people see what we post, and when they do, they often scroll right past and keep their eyes—and nervous systems—tethered to the very screens already contributing to our collective isolation. Research in psychology and neuroscience consistently links chronic screen engagement to elevated stress, fragmented attention, and reduced felt social connection, even when interactions appear "social."[9]

In this light, posting can unintentionally reinforce the disconnection it seeks to solve. This is why gathering in small groups and consistently showing up with friends in real life remains so critical to sharing in a way that reveals your care. Face-to-face presence regulates the nervous system, restores emotional safety, and reminds us that the most enduring form of influence is not digital reach, but relational depth. It's easier to share and to care in person.

In an ecosystem crowded with artificial influence, the most meaningful impact may no longer be broadcast at scale, but embodied quietly—in small rooms, unhurried conversations, and moments of presence where attention is fully human. That's why authentic vulnerability helps create connection and build trust.

Spice Levels

As we conclude this chapter, I want to return to the general idea of *if you really knew me*. Shallow or deep, the desire to be known and the willingness to let yourself be known is the key to sharing connection with others.

In terms of the exercise itself, sometimes at larger conferences, the sponsoring organization will create a huge, physical *if you really knew me* wall where individual conference attendees can write something for everyone else to see.

Sometimes, I like to hang out near the board to connect with people. At one particular conference, I engaged the one guy who had just written something. "I haven't read what you wrote yet," I said. "Do you mind sharing what it is?"

As it turned out, he was supposed to be on one of the planes that crashed into the towers of the World Trade Center on September 11, 2001. It was one of the craziest and most vulnerable things anyone had ever shared in this exercise. After he told me, his face became sullen and stoic. I leaned in and asked him to share what he was feeling.

The day before his flight, a last-minute change in assignment at his company moved his responsibilities to a different client, which meant that someone more senior went on the trip in his place. For 25 years and counting, he had lived with survivor's guilt. We kept talking for a while and learned so much about each other. I didn't take all his pain away, but I do feel that both of our lives were better off because of our connection.

Vulnerability was the key to our meaningful moment. In this case, it was deep, but as we have discovered, it can also be lighter. I like to look at vulnerability as a spice: it can be mild, medium, or hot. If you share that you're left-handed, that's pretty mild. If you share that you grew up in a broken home and your parents are divorced, that's more like medium. If you share that you have lived a quarter-of-a-century with chronic survivors' guilt because you were supposed to be on a plane that crashed into the twin towers, that's spicier. There is no wrong level of spice.

Any level of connection can serve to remind us that we stand on more common ground than we realize. There is a real person behind every Instagram and LinkedIn profile, a human beneath all the external polish, business or formal attire, and perfect profile-pic smile. From the Delta diaries to *if you really knew me* exercise at conferences, if we are intentional, we can draw out of people that which is more organic, authentic, and life-giving.

In fact, we're in danger of missing these intentional person-to-person connections based on mutual struggle. We are becoming more likely to share our issues and ask questions of ChatGPT than real people. We need dialogue and connection—and AI gives us just enough of it to lull us into a false sense of connection. Is there anything wrong with connecting with AI? Not morally, I suppose. But you can never do the *if you really knew me* exercise with ChatGPT. It doesn't share the human experience.

The upside to human connection is shared humanity. If you share that you struggle with depression, a human can share that they have struggled with depression as well—and offer insights to how they have coped and worked through it. They can suggest a counselor or a support group not from a sophisticated web search; rather, they can tell you what has helped in their own real, human life. Plus, such interactions can also turn into long-term closeness and connection through texts, phone calls, and shared meals.

All this versus "Hey, Chat, I'm feeling depressed."

Yes, Chat can offer a great list of insights and resources. This can be a really good thing. The issue is not the information, but the ongoing encouragement required to walk out the information away from isolation. Human connection positions us for sustained momentum rather than a temporary information dump. The information may be helpful and accurate, but unless it ultimately connects you to a human—a therapist, counselor, recovery group, support group, or even just a friend—you will be left to implement in isolation.

If you really knew me—well, now that you're really coming to know me—then you're realizing that my life experiences have taught me, often the hard way, that we must seek and embrace shared experiences and shared stories. We must share life's trials and successes with other people who are actually alive. All this strengthens the human fabric connecting us to one another in meaningful ways.

Reflection

When you quietly complete the sentence "If you really knew me . . . ," what would you share?

10 Conflict and Connection

"At the core of all anger is a need that is not being met."

—Marshall Rosenberg

If you really knew me, you'd know I did not go to the gym for conflict resolution.

I went for the sauna.

But lately, the locker room has become a bit of a classroom for me. Not because I am looking for lessons, but because life has a way of bringing them to you when you are paying attention.

Two moments, just one week apart, reminded me of something I am still learning in real time:

Conflict is inevitable.
Connection is optional.
Presence is the difference.

Locker Room Lesson 1: Lower the Heat

I stepped out of the sauna in my towel, still dripping wet, and immediately felt tension.

A man in his fifties stood across from four high school seniors, full of energy and emotion. Voices were rising. Shoulders were squared. You could feel it in the air.

We were one comment away from something everyone would regret.

Much to my surprise, without hesitation, I stepped right in between them and firmly said, "Where is the peace?"

Silence.

I smiled this time and said it again, more softly.

"Where is the peace?"

I turned to one of the younger guys and asked him what was going on.

He said, frustrated, "The older man thinks we opened his locker to take his stuff."

The tension started to rise again, so I offered something simple.

"The wisest person in an argument is the first one to acknowledge the other person's perspective and mirror it back to them."

The young man nodded and turned to the older gentleman.

"I understand why you're frustrated. One of us may have opened your locker by accident. That wasn't our intent. We're sorry."

The older man paused.

"Thank you. Acknowledgment was all I was looking for."

Just like that, the temperature dropped.

A few of the younger guys started to chime in again, ready to restart the argument. I turned and gave them a look.

"Let's keep moving toward peace, boys."

Moments later, the man walked out. It was over.

I turned back to the group and said, "I've learned this the hard way with my wife, my kids, and at work. Disagreements will happen. But when things start heating up, you need to find a way to lower the heat. The best way to do that is to lower your voice and stop talking."

They nodded. You could feel the room relax.

Connection replaced conflict.

On the drive home, two thoughts stayed with me.

First, leadership often looks like stepping into moments that aren't yours, but are yours to influence.

It's easy to stay out of it and think, "It's not my business. I don't need to get involved."

But sometimes the most powerful thing you can do is step into the middle.

Second, even though I interrupted, I didn't really have any skin in the game. Pun intended, as I was still soaking wet from the sauna.

But maybe that's the point.

Sometimes the people best positioned to bring peace are the ones who aren't trying to win.

Locker Room Lesson 2: Raise the Standard

A week later, I returned for a quick workout before heading home to make breakfast for dinner with the kids.

I wasn't especially motivated, so I did what I usually do. I put on a sermon, walked a mile, lifted a bit, and then made my way into the sauna.

When I walked into the sauna, it was packed. Five guys, mid-twenties to mid-forties. I found a small opening between two men on the top row. Sitting between them was an *Automotive News* newspaper that had clearly been there since earlier that morning.

I asked if anyone was reading it.

"Nope," one of them said.

I picked it up and sat down in the only dry spot left.

As I flipped through it, a conversation started.

One guy joked, "I've been in the auto industry for 29 years . . . and I've got 11 more years left on my life sentence."

We all laughed.

Another guy shared that he had gotten out of automotive and moved into the grocery business.

Curious, I asked, "Oh, really? Do you own a grocery store?"

"Nope."

"So what do you do? Are you a manager or a cashier?"

"Nope."

I paused, trying to understand.

"So what do you actually do? Are you a bagger?"

He paused, then said, "I like to bag women."

The comment came out of nowhere.

And if I'm honest, it didn't sit right.

I didn't confront him. I didn't laugh along. I just gave a look that probably said, "that didn't land."

The two younger guys chuckled.

I left the sauna and stepped into the steam room next door.

Thankfully, I was the only one in there. I paced back and forth and prayed, something I often do when I have the room to myself.

But I couldn't quite shake what he said.

Not because I've never said something immature. I have. Trust me. I lived in a fraternity house with 55 guys.

But it felt off. Out of place. Like something said more for the room than from the person.

After a few minutes, I stepped out, grabbed my towel, and got ready to head home.

But as soon as I did, something unexpected happened.

The same guy walked up to me.

"Hey," he said. "I want to apologize. I'm happily married. I respect women. I don't even know why I said that."

I looked at him and said, "I really appreciate you saying that."

Then I added, "I'm guessing you could sense your comment didn't land with me, but it means a lot that you came back."

He nodded.

Before he left, I said, "You know, sometimes in a locker room like that, especially around guys half our age, it's easy to slip back into old versions of ourselves."

He paused, then smiled.

We both smiled.

And that was it.

No confrontation. No correction.

Just presence.

And somehow, that was enough to create reflection.

A moment of conviction.

A moment of repair.

What I experienced in those two moments isn't random—it's actually something we see play out in human behavior all the time.

The Lesson Beneath the Steam

There is a reason both of these moments mattered.

And it is bigger than the locker room.

In psychology, it is often referred to as *regression*, when we unconsciously revert to earlier behaviors in certain environments.[1]

There is also something called *social contagion*, in which attitudes and behaviors spread through a group without us even realizing it.[2]

And maybe most simply: we tend to rise or fall to the level of the room we are in.

Especially when we are trying, consciously or not, to belong.

Sometimes that means escalating.

Sometimes that means staying silent.

Sometimes that means becoming a slightly lesser version of ourselves just to fit in.

But these moments reminded me of something else.

We also have the ability to raise the standard of the room, without raising our voice.

Now imagine those same dynamics—tension, influence, belonging, no longer confined to a locker room, but amplified across a screen.

The Digital Locker Room

Dr. Jared Cooney Horvath, a cognitive neuroscientist with research experience at Harvard, has found something concerning.

For the first time in modern history, this generation (Gen Z) is declining in attention, memory, and cognitive performance. Not because they are less capable, but because the environments shaping them are different.[3]

Faster. Louder. More stimulating. Less relational.

We are raising a generation in what feels like a digital locker room.

I see it in our friends who have teenage boys. For the most part, they are all great young men who I enjoy being around and am eager to see the men they become.

And yet, they are growing up in the thick of what I've started to call the three Gs: Gaming. Gambling. Grumbling.

Not because they chose it, but because it found them.

Gaming isn't just play anymore. It's immersive, endless, and often designed to keep you engaged for hours at a time. Wins are instant. Losses are recoverable. There's always another level, another match, another reason to stay.[4]

Gambling is no longer confined to casinos. It's woven into the platforms they already use. Sports betting, cryptocurrency chasing, loot boxes, and reward-based systems are showing up in their feeds and games—often without them even searching for it.[5]

And then there's grumbling.

Not loud complaining. Not full-on rebellion.

But a low-grade, constant distraction.

A drifting of attention.

A shortening of patience.

A subtle frustration that shows up when real life doesn't move at the speed of a screen.

It's what happens when the brain gets used to high stimulation and then has to return to ordinary moments—conversation, conflict, waiting, listening.[6]

And when you combine declining attention with constant stimulation and reward-driven environments, something shifts.

You don't just get distraction.

You get distorted conflict.[7]

Shorter fuses.

Quicker reactions.

Less capacity to sit in tension, to listen, to understand.

I notice this in preteen kids when I coach soccer. I have the joy of coaching a bunch of fifth- and sixth-grade students who love to play soccer. I try my best to not only teach them soccer skills they can use on the field, but also life skills they can use to build their character off the field.

But if I'm being honest, they, too, are teaching me lessons. One of them happened last year.

Memes, Mirror Neurons, and Brain Rot (the Okay Kind)

At the time of this writing, a certain phenomenon is burning through the internet based on the number combination 6–7. Yes, I realize that current readers will likely know exactly what I'm talking about, but if you're reading this in the near or distant future, you may wonder what in the world I'm talking about. If it makes you feel any better, just know those of us living this out in real time are also wondering what in the world we're talking about. Regardless, you don't have to be experiencing it to understand its application to shared connection.

On the soccer field, I first encountered it when we would do stretches and count from 1 to 10. When we reached six and seven, a dozen middle schoolers would yell out the numbers and burst out laughing. It happened every single time and every single time, I was confused, which by the way, is the point.

The 6–7 meme emerged in early 2025 from a rapper's song and then gained traction through certain TikTok accounts. Soon, there was an accompanying hand gesture—a palms-up, seesaw motion. By March 2025, a young man became the meme's unofficial mascot when a video of him enthusiastically shouting "six seven!" at a basketball game went viral. The phrase—which means essentially nothing—became a constant distraction in classrooms, with teachers reporting kids shouting it whenever page 67 appeared, the clock showed 6:07, or simply for no reason at all. Dictionary.com named *67* its word of the year.

The thing is, the expression really means nothing at all, but using it makes kids feel like they're part of an inside joke—and, most importantly, a joke delivered at the adults' expense. Kids feel most united when they are in on something that we, the ones in charge, can never fully understand—after all, there is no explanation. Within weeks, this silly phrase became social glue: it bonded kids to one another and metaphorically glued the adults to our chairs. It is a secret prank being conducted in broad daylight—or should I say, broad phone light.

The 6–7 meme itself was born out of what social scientists called *brain rot*. Yes, it's not the most beautiful phrase, but it represents a growing genre of internet language that constitute a stream of absurd memes, sounds, inside jokes, and phrases that make no sense on their own. However, when people experience them together, they're funny, repeatable, and socially contagious. Brain rot content is so repetitive, nonsensical, or silly that it gets stuck in your head and becomes a shared experience.

To be clear, brain rot is not usually considered to be something positive, mainly because it becomes people's only methodology of interacting with the world. I'm not encouraging it; I'm simply making an observation about the power of shared experiences, regardless of their meaning or depth. Even back in the 1980s and 1990s, we developed viral phrases that bonded us, generally against the awareness of the adults. We used the word *bad* to describe things that were really good. We would tell crazy stories and then negate them by yelling "not!" or "psyche!"

From then to now, brain rot is not about intellect. It's about emotion, humor, ease, and belonging. The phrase 6–7 is meaningless on the surface, but it's meaningful because everyone's in on it. And in a world full of tension and digital noise, kids are using brain rot slang as a way to create some sense of the connection they so desperately desire. It lowers the stakes and tightens bonds over shared smiles. The heart of this meme peeks back to the science behind sharing, and specifically to the neuroscientific discovery of mirror neurons.

Mirror neurons are brain cells that fire on two fronts: when I perform an action and when I observe *someone else* performing that same action. They came to the forefront of popular science by accident in the 1990s by Italian neuroscientists who were studying macaque monkeys at the University of Parma. Long story short, while a monkey had electrodes to its prefrontal cortex, a scientist reached for something to eat during a break in the research. When he did, the monkey's neurons fired, even though the monkey itself wasn't reaching for the food. As they more closely examined the phenomenon, they found that the same cells activated by the monkey reaching for something also activated when the monkey simply watched someone else reaching.[8]

Ironically, this also helps explain all this 6–7 monkey business today.

We all know this to be true in other ways. If we see someone yawn, we can't help but yawn ourselves. If someone smiles at us in the grocery store, we smile in return. And when one kid laughs at 6–7, every other kid laughs, too. Though there is some debate about the potential extent of the implications of mirror neurons, they do offer at least one explanation for our tendency to imitate behaviors we observe in others, especially when these behaviors are socially charged or socially rewarded. Kids see the 6–7 behaviors. Their neurons fire. The behavior replicates. Adults roll their eyes.

Everyone wins—well, except the adults.

That's the power of shared experience, even when the topic is nonsensical. Connection that is light and quick can also still be disarming and effective. Even goofy little rituals can lay the first layer for deeper truths. Obviously, my goal is that we learn to go deeper, but the power of connection reveals itself in all forms. We are all craving something to belong to. And with as divisive as the internet and social media can become, I believe humor to be one of the fastest bonds to creating social connections.

In a world full of noise, kids found this simple moment that brought them together. Finding any common ground is one of the fastest ways to build connection, so whether you're in a meeting, picking up your son or daughter from soccer, or finding yourself in a social gathering that feels stiff and sterile, look for anything that you can share. A smile. A moment. A cultural inside joke.

While I warn against brain rot as your predominant method of interaction, I do give you permission to use it sparingly with boundaries and parameters. Just don't use it exclusively and don't use it alone. Sometimes conflict is healthy and can be necessary to teach and learn a lesson. And while these shared moments that I just mentioned can create connection, they also reveal something deeper about how we handle tension.

Avoidance Versus Escalation

My friend Dan recently shared a line that stopped me in my tracks: "Every time you avoid conflict, you abandon yourself."

That's real.

But here's what I'm learning.

In today's world, we're not just avoiding conflict.

We're accelerating it.

We either avoid, explode, or perform.

Rarely do we stay present long enough and lean into the messy middle. Just like I felt called to in the locker room.

The Messy Middle: Presence

Presence does not avoid conflict.

Presence does not escalate conflict.

Presence transforms it.

It looks like lowering your voice when others raise theirs.

It looks like acknowledging before arguing.

It looks like holding your ground without hardening your heart.

In the locker room, presence created peace.

In the sauna, presence created reflection.

In the digital world, presence may be the most important skill we can relearn.

So how do we live this out consistently?

Not just in a locker room. Not just in a moment of tension. But in our homes, our workplaces, and the everyday interactions that shape our lives.

Because the truth is, presence is powerful, but it is also practiced.

Over time, I began to notice that the moments when connection replaced conflict were not random. They were rooted in a set of inner postures and habits that could be developed.

That's what led me to a simple framework I now call the GIFTS model.

We'll explore that framework next, but for now, it's worth pausing here.

Final Reflection

In a world that escalates quickly, choose to be a person who brings the peace.

I still think about those four Gen Z young men in the locker room.

In that moment, I didn't teach the men in the locker room how to win an argument.

I simply showed them how to lower the heat.

My hope is that something in that moment stayed with them.

That it gave them a little more confidence, a little more awareness, and a different way to respond the next time tension rises—whether it's in a locker room or in the digital locker room they live in every day.

Ronald Reagan once said, "Peace is not the absence of conflict, but the ability to handle conflict by peaceful means."[9]

And more often than not, presence is where peace begins.

Reflection

Where in your life is there tension that you've been walking around instead of walking into?

What if your role is not to fix it, but to bring your presence into it?

11 The GIFTS Model

"The ultimate meaning of life is to give, not to get."

—**Wayne Dyer**

As our time in these pages comes to a close, I want to leave you with the most practical way I know to apply the principles of being a gift of connection in your own world. Over the past 15 years, I've had the privilege of meeting thousands of people—from CEOs to cashiers, parents to pastors, and speakers to strangers on the street. Some bore the title of *leader*. Others did not. Honestly, this made no difference because each of them still had had something in common. Something unforgettable. It wasn't their charisma or confidence that stood out. It was something quieter. More intentional. Deep in their bones. What was it?

They each had moments—even if only brief ones—when *their presence broke through the noise*. They made someone else feel seen, valued, or understood—and that someone was often me. Their value shone bright through the collective human shadow that threatens to eclipse us all. These moments have stuck with me and as I have pondered them, I have noticed patterns.

These people carried qualities that restored connection not just with others but also with themselves. I began calling them the GIFTS of connection:

- Grace
- Influence
- Focus
- Trust
- Sensitivity

These aren't personality traits. They're *presence traits*. Anyone can grow them. They help us show up more fully, first with ourselves, then with each other.

You don't need to master all five overnight, but I believe we all carry these GIFTS inside us. When we practice them with intention, we create the kind of connection that heals, energizes, and transforms.

This chapter will tell a few stories of people I've met who embodied these traits. You'll meet a kindergarten teacher, a hotel lost-and-found coordinator, an unsuspecting neighbor, a father of five boys, and a man in his eighties receiving a lifetime achievement award.

Each of them models one of these traits in a way that's raw, real, and unforgettable. Each of them shows each of us who we can be if we are willing to unwrap and share the gift of ourselves with others.

Avocados and Grace—(GIFTS)

Morning routines are important for all of us, but especially when you have younger kids. Routines set the day into comforting motion, enabling everyone to organize what lies ahead in the new day.

When my daughter, Mila, was in kindergarten, I came down early as usual to pour my steaming cup of coffee and begin readying everything for the day. But before I could even lay out the cereal for the snoozing munchkins upstairs, Mila suddenly appeared, coming down fully dressed with her hair already in a ponytail. To say the least, this was *not* in our routine.

"Hey kiddo, you're up extra early. How did you sleep?" I began making her cereal as she climbed up in a chair at the kitchen island.

"Daddy, I get to be the line leader today!" she beamed.

I could tell she had so much more she wanted to share, so I took the bait. "That's really great, Mila! Now, what exactly does the line leader do?"

She took a bite of cereal and pondered my question. "Uh, I get to lead the line." It was a statement, but it sounded more like a question.

"Right," I replied. "Of course. But are there other responsibilities?"

That question really seemed to do something inside her little head. After a few seconds, she looked me straight in the eyes and, I kid you not, she said, "Dad, I don't have enough time to tell you all of the responsibilities of the line leader." It took everything within me to contain the laughter, but I didn't want to embarrass her. Also, I wondered where she got so much spunk?

The rest of the morning was fairly normal. I dropped the kids off at school and went about my work day. Then lo and behold, an email popped into my inbox right before lunch. It was from Mila's teacher, Mrs. Wilkie, with the subject "Line Leader."

Ruh-roh, Raggy.

In my mind, I imagined the worst. She had one job to do and she had blown it. She was not going to graduate kindergarten. Do not pass go. Do not collect $200. No doubt, a life of crime and prison were not far behind—a tale as old as time.

The teacher went on to share that one of the responsibilities of the line leader was to pray before snack time. Now, despite her sweet little spunkiness at home, Mila is actually rather shy. Yet, with courage, she had stood up in front of all of her classmates who were sitting cross-legged on the floor, prepping their graham crackers, popcorn, apple slices, and the like. Mila bowed her head, folded her hands, and began to utter a prayer she had prayed a thousand times in her short life.

"God our Father . . ."

Only, that's not what came out. The syllables and diction were almost identical, but unfortunately, the words were not. Instead of "God our Father," Mila confidently prayed, "A-vo-cado . . ."

To her defense, Mila does come from an environment rife with fruits and veggies; albeit, we don't generally pray to them. Poor Mila immediately heard herself and turned a shade of red preserved for only the rosiest of little cheeks.

It happens. Humans mess up the easiest of things. We all have that story we can return to in our minds that leads to an involuntary pit in our stomachs or an audible groan. *What was I thinking?* To be human is to need grace. To need grace is to need a conduit—that is, someone aware and willing to show it. Thankfully, Mrs. Wilkie was there.

Without making a big deal, Mrs. Wilkie stifled her own laughter, saving it for later in the day. Instead, she smiled, gently quieted the classroom snickers, and said, "It's okay. Try again, my dear." The rest of Mila's prayer went off without a hitch or the deification of any other foods. With "cheeses" sounding so much like "Jesus," I'd say we really dodged a mullet. (We eat a lot of fish, too.)

Mila was simply nervous and overwhelmed by all of the responsibilities of the line leader—after all, we know the job was pretty big in her sweet little head. Have you ever been there? I sure have. We're not alone.

During the pandemic, I was commissioned to organize a very simple research study of 3,000 people across 30 organizations, inviting participants to answer questions about their emotional and digital health. It was a simple five-question survey.

In one of the questions, I asked participants to use one word to describe their week. The commonalities of the results were staggering—*overwhelmed*, *anxious*, *stressed*, and *tired* were the top responses. Even when the studies aren't as formal, I still get similar answers when I poll audiences at live events.

Another significant finding from our research was that those who engaged in 25 or more video meetings each week—Microsoft Teams, Zoom, Google Meets, and so on—were twice as likely to report poor emotional health. Let that sink in. Such a work life is the norm for millions of people today. Is the answer to eliminate such things? Let's be honest—people were overwhelmed before these tools became commonplace. Yes, we do need some things to be pared back or removed, but more importantly, we need something else added in greater quantities: grace.

One of my past clients are the folks at Henry Ford Health, one of the largest hospital groups in Michigan, serving the Detroit Lions and millions of people across the state. One of their stated corporate mentalities is "grace and grit." They work with enough hurting people and enough healthcare professionals giving their daily lives to meet these endless needs that they know grace is necessary for human flourishing.

Grace is not the *only* thing we need, but it is always the *first* thing.

I believe grace is an essential need for the modern-day workplace—and any connection, for that matter. You need it on the days when you feel sharp and ready for the day's challenges just as much as you need it on the days when the first thing out of your mouth is "avocado." If we can just give people a break instead of always holding them to the fire, we foster the very thing we all need the most.

Grace lived out in practical conversations is always a matter of tone, truth, and timing. I once interviewed a foreman who shared extensively about his role in managing both physical and psychological safety on the jobsite. Most of us only think of the physical side. He once had a worker who never wore his safety glasses without being told to do so. Days passed of reminder after reminder to the point that the foreman was becoming highly frustrated.

On yet another morning, the foreman began to approach the man again when he was intercepted by another coworker. "Take it easy on him, boss," the worker said. "He's going through a bad divorce right now." Turns out, like every one of us, there is almost always a reason behind what we're doing or not doing. It just takes a little patient grace to find it.

The foreman approached the man, but this time, he did so with gentleness. "Hey man, why aren't your glasses on?" His tone was different, which created a different reaction. "I'm sorry, boss," the worker replied, "I haven't slept in days and I keep forgetting."

This interaction led to the two men taking a walk around the jobsite as the foreman listened to his coworker's problems and shared about his own painful divorce five years earlier. By the end, they knew each other well enough to even toss around some jokes. Tone, truth, and timing—a shift in tone had led to painful truth and perfect timing for fresh empathy that had not been there before. The only difference was grace.

After that, not only did the two men share a deeper connection but the worker also had no trouble remembering to wear his safety glasses. You are not in control of circumstances or people, but you are in control of how you show up in people's circumstances—and in every instance, grace goes a long way to help foster real connection.

Pink Unicorns and Influence—(GIFTS)

You have influence. You may not feel it, but it's there. Being alive is the only condition of influence. Yes, some people may influence more people than others, but we all influence someone in some way. In *The Gift of Influence*, Tommy Spalding paints an incredible picture by pointing out how at the end of your life, you'll have had a chance to influence over 80,000 people, the same capacity of many NFL stadiums.[1] You can't have a funeral large enough to hold that many, but real influence isn't about what people say about you at the end. Real influence is about how you connect with people in real, authentic ways today.

In this respect, when you connect rightly, you lead with influence even if you don't fancy yourself much of a leader. Real leaders don't always have the corner offices, give speeches, or garner national followings. As John Maxwell famously writes, "The true measure of leadership is influence—nothing more, nothing less."[2] Teachers, coaches, parents, and friends all have the potential to lead in this world by using connection as their path to influence that makes a difference.

When I think of this kind of influence, I think of a woman named Penny. Penny worked at the Boyne Mountain Ski and Golf Resort in beautiful Boyne Falls in northern Michigan. Our family spent three days there on the slopes, somehow coming home with no injuries. It is a picturesque locale—the stuff winter Hallmark movies are made of. We enjoyed our little neck of the 300-room resort, along with all the fine eateries and all the hot chocolate we could drink. When the trip ended, I packed up and loaded all the boots, bags, and belongings into our minivan, my heart still blissfully skiing somewhere up on that mountain.

About two hours into our four-hour drive home, I heard the first peep from the tired crew in the back of the van. It was Mila. "Hey, Dad? Do you know where my pink unicorn is?" Suddenly, I was sucked out of my body into some sort of ethereal state of subconscious panic. From this dark alternate reality, I hovered over time and space, able to revisit the morning and visualize everything I had packed. In my soul, I knew I had not packed the pink unicorn. I didn't want it to be true, but soon tears filled the car—and Mila cried some, too.

The pink unicorn was a Ostach family heirloom, a staple in Mila's life since the day she was born. She had slept with it every day since she was an infant. As you can imagine, at five years old, her grief was real as it gets.

Regardless, we were too far on the road to turn back at that point. But I did assure her I would call the resort immediately. I was transferred to the lost and found department, which while on hold, I pictured as this gigantic warehouse of left-handed boots, left-handed gloves, empty wallets, sunglasses, ski poles, and all the things that people leave behind at a ski resort. Finally, I reached a lady named Penny.

Penny had worked in the lost and found department for over 18 years. In her voice, there was a sense of kindness and dedication. She assured me they would look high and low for the pink unicorn. She even joked that they were going to bring in a sketch artist to make sure we had the correct unicorn.

Penny called me back an hour later to let me know that the full resort staff had been alerted to the search. It sounded promising, so I told Mila that before we would get home, Penny would no doubt call me to let me know the unicorn had been found. I meant well, but that was a big mistake.

Weeks passed and I had many calls with Penny, but to my chagrin, there was no unicorn. Mila experimented holding other stuffed animals in the bed, but she wasn't at peace. So I kept calling Penny for six weeks straight. I assumed that would bother her, but it didn't—she was pleasant. But finally, after I offered to come back up to the resort and expand the search grid myself, complete with a pack of stuffed bloodhounds to help, Penny had the decency to tell me straight. She had been in the missing stuffed animals business for a long time. She'd seen some bad stuff.

The pink unicorn was gone.

We all mourned, but time marched on until signs of spring began to appear. If you live in the Midwest, you begin wearing shorts when it's 50 degrees outside. It's your way of hurrying the winter away. On just such a briskly mild Friday night, the doorbell rang. It was a UPS driver with a package. When I opened it, I saw a handwritten sticky note that read "Dear Mila, thank you for letting me stay at Boyne Mountain for a few more weeks. I rode the chairlift. It was fun. So was the water park. I missed you though, and I was ready to come home!" Then I unwrapped the tissue paper to reveal the pink unicorn. The whole family literally rejoiced and Mila began bouncing off the walls.

I keep a picture of Mila and the unicorn to look at on days when I'm feeling down. It reminds me of the precious gift of reconciliation, when something you've lost is restored. Penny gave us that feeling. She influenced us in ways we never expected. I marveled that she remembered my daughter's name and took the time to make a child's reunion with her stuffed animal so special.

I called Penny and told her how grateful we were, and that she had been such a positive influence on our entire family. In her humility, she said she was just doing her job. But we've all been enough places to know that everyone doesn't do their job with that level of kindness, presence, and intentionality. The way she did her normal job was highly influential.

The way you live your normal life can be highly influential as well. Your influence is something to be cultivated and given away. For years to come, the story of Penny and the pink unicorn was used by the resort company's leadership to celebrate great customer service in their trainings to other employees. But somehow, I know that's not why Penny did it. You don't work somewhere as long as she had for just the "atta boy" from the boss. No, she did what she did because she knew who she wanted to be: an influencer. Consequently, her positive embodiment of the term *influencer* had nothing to do with online views or likes. It rarely does.

I don't know what you spend your days doing, but I do know there is a football stadium of people waiting for each of us to use the gift of presence to pursue connection and influence the world around us for the better. All it takes is the willingness to keep reaching outside yourself for the good of others.

Stolen Wi-Fi and Focus—(GIFTS)

Early in my speaking career, we moved into a new home. Back then, I was doing a ton of virtual events and one day, I was set to speak at the largest virtual event of my career up to that point. I was going to speak over Zoom to about 1,500 professional team members around the country who worked at my largest client, Rocket Mortgage, based in Detroit.

I was hired to deliver a one-hour keynote session about mental health awareness. I decided to make the event more creative by partnering with an incredible musician friend named Bob Mervak. We were going to alternate between my stories and his songs to entertain and inform the call attendees about how the music of their mind influences their mindset and their work product. We had successfully pulled off this dual-approach presentation several times in person, but we had never tried it virtually.

What could go wrong?

We were both very excited because it was a huge opportunity. Earlier in the day, we logged on for a tech check, which meant we tried out our cameras, microphones, and internet connection. Everything went off without a hitch. I spent the next few hours practicing my speech and going over my notes. I was ready—this was going to be great!

The moment finally came. I logged on and watched as hundreds on hundreds of little squares began popping up on my screen. This was it! After a few minutes, the emcee of the event began to introduce Bob and I. As he came to the last sentence of my introduction, I kid you not, my internet froze.

I'll take existential crisis for $1,000, Alex.

I had done many events in the past, but this had never happened before—and boy, did it pick a doozy of a time. However, I had also prepared for such contingencies with backup generators, routers, and the like. None of it mattered or seemed to work. The internet said no and I began to flip out.

My Zoom wouldn't work, but my texts sure did. Bob began blowing up my phone, wondering where I was. I immediately called the event planner and apologized. I told him I was going to restart everything and get back to him. It took about five minutes for the entire sequence. Still, I got nothing.

Cue panic, round two.

As insult and injury kept alternating their cruel additions, I had a crazy idea that led to me getting on a bicycle with my laptop. I peddled furiously like the Wicked Witch of the West (sorry, Elphaba) down the dirt road to my neighbor's house. I didn't really know him that well, but he was older and his kids were out of the house already. I had used his internet for a business call a few months before when we were having work done at our house. I peddled like a madman, but alas, on arrival at my destination, I found that he wasn't home.

Houston, we had a problem like 10 minutes ago—now we're fully crashing and burning.

I texted Bob and told him just to start playing "Don't Stop Believing" by Journey on his keyboard to fill the dead space, even though, ironically, I had stopped believing. I was blowing my chance to connect with the team members from my biggest client. I could feel the opportunity slipping away. But just as I began to wave the white flag of defeat, I took a deep breath. Suddenly, I thought of a way to pivot. I remembered that my neighbor's Wi-Fi credentials were still saved on my laptop. This could work.

From a patio-style rocking chair, I logged on and went live from my neighbor's porch. Thankfully, the porch was shaded at that time of day, so I was able to see my laptop screen with no problems. Bob ended his 13th chorus of "Don't Stop Believing" and I did my best to jump into my presentation as seamlessly as possible, as if nothing had happened.

It worked! Suddenly, the presentation was actually going well. Just then, I had a thought: what if my neighbor comes home and finds me on his porch, uninvited, waving my hands in front of my laptop as I pirate his internet. Again, we really didn't know each other that well. Thankfully, he did not show up during the remainder of my 55-minute presentation. It was the perfect crime.

In the end, there was little disruption to my client's expectations. Yes, I had been a little panicked, but the best antidote to panic is focus on your commitment to presence. Never give up on being present and sharing your gift of connection, even when things don't go according to plan. I call this *situational presence*: adapting the process and commitment to connecting with others to the circumstances at hand. After all, if you wait for perfect conditions, you'll never connect with anyone. Situational presence requires focus.

Most of us are not surgeons, but they know a little about pivoting on the fly to achieve a critical goal. In a moment when things don't go according to plan, they have to use their training, education, imagination, and sheer instinct to make intentional adjustments. The stakes are too high not to try. They have to find focus when everything around them is trying to rob them of it.

When sharing the gift of yourself with others, it won't always go according to plan. It is easy to give up or allow yourself to roam into distraction or anxiousness instead of connection. Part of this has to do with where your head is at given the circumstances or environment around you. Neuroscientist Dr. Dan Siegel popularized the concepts of the *upstairs brain* and *downstairs brain*. When we feel threatened or overwhelmed, we shift to the downstairs brain, which is more reactive as inner fight-or-flight responses eclipse clear thinking and response.

The goal is to get back to the upstairs brain located in the prefrontal cortex. Here, we can remain calm and engage with more emotional and cognitive clarity.[3]

One way to make this shift back to the upstairs brain is through conscious breathing, which can help you navigate whatever distraction is competing for your focus. When stress hijacks your focus or emotions, your breath can bring you back. Techniques like STAR breathing, balloon breathing, pretzel breathing, and faucet breathing are great examples of methods designed to redirect breath back to the place it benefits your brain, leading you from reactive to receptive.

STAR breath is based on the acronym: *smile, take a deep breath, and relax*. The technique involves taking slow, deep breaths in through the nose, pausing briefly, and then exhaling slowly through the mouth while consciously attempting to relax your body. The physical act of smiling actually sends calming signals to your brain.[4]

Balloon breathing involves interlacing your fingers with the palm of your hands on top of your head. As you inhale deeply through the nose, raise your arms overhead as if you are inflating an invisible balloon. When the "balloon" is fully inflated, slowly exhale while lowering your arms, letting the air escaping from the balloon, making a sound like you are blowing raspberries. These movements help you take slow, deep breaths using your diaphragm.[5]

To try the pretzel breathing technique, extend your arms straight out in front of you, palms facing outward. Then, crosses one hand over the other and interlace your fingers. Next, fold your hands inward toward your chest (creating a pretzel shape with your arms). Crossing your ankles and placing your tongue on the roof of your mouth completes the posture. Now, breathe in slowly through the nose while briefly holding this position, then exhale out your mouth while extending your arms back outward. This technique provides deep proprioceptive input—it's kind of like giving yourself a hug.[6]

Finally, faucet breathing (also known as drain breathing) is a technique that uses the imagery of draining stress out of the body like water from a faucet. Extend your arms out to the sides at shoulder height (making a *T* shape), curling your hands into fists. Then, tighten all the muscles in your face, shoulders, arms, and hands while inhaling deeply through the nose. As you exhale through your mouth, make a "ssshhh" sound as you simultaneously relax all your muscles as your arms drop. Try to visualize all the tension, worry, and stress draining out of your body.[7]

Connection takes focus, but as we have learned, focus is not usually a matter of only thinking harder. Our bodies are connected to our brains so the path to focus comes best through a wholistic physiological approach. Regardless of how we get there, it takes focus to keep seeking creative ways to connect with others, even when it's not convenient. From a mental and societal health standpoint, the stakes are too high not to connect. We have to keep pushing through what divides us to find those commonalities that connect us—even if we have to steal our neighbor's Wi-Fi to do it.

As it were.

Eagles and Trust—(GIFTS)

I love eagles. In fact, I don't know anyone who doesn't at least admire these majestic creatures. Yes, Benjamin Franklin lamented that the turkey wasn't named our national bird, but I'm guessing that was before he invented bifocals—because he obviously wasn't seeing things clearly. That's the only explanation.

Once when I was presenting at a conference, I was preceded by a speaker named Sam Glenn, also known as *the attitude guy*. He's a motivational speaker and performance artist who paints live on stage during his keynote presentations. Illustrating what he calls *the art of inspiration*, I was blown away to watch Sam paint a huge eagle on a canvas in less than 20 minutes. His whole presentation was a thing of beauty.

Not only did I feel privileged to be in the audience but I was also a little nervous because my keynote was just a bunch of slides and pictures with no live painting. As I contemplated adding a last-minute fire-juggling routine and scanned the backstage for any spare cans of kerosene, the emcee of the conference took the podium and announced they were about to auction off Sam's eagle painting for charity.

I was intrigued because, let me tell you, I loved this painting. It was four feet high and four feet wide, a gigantic canvas of beauty and grandeur. Sure, my wife usually handles all our interior decorating. And sure, we didn't have an empty wall big enough for something this massive. Regardless, I wanted it.

Early bidding began and before I knew it, my hand had raised itself in the air, as if I had nothing to do with it. Yeah, that's what I would tell my wife when I showed up back home with his gargantuan avian wonder.

As the bidding went higher and higher, so did my rebellious hand, over and over again. Note that I don't have a lot of discretional income, especially at this point in my life. Our walls and our wallets weren't big enough for this eagle painting, but it was so glorious that I couldn't stop bidding. Soon, the price had soared into eagle territory of thousands of dollars. But the truth is, I no longer wanted to hang it on my wall. My heart was hiding a secret mission for this eagle, one that would help someone else.

The bidding came down to me and one other guy in the crowd. The bid kept going higher and higher to the point that somewhere in this high-stakes standoff, my brain overrode my hand, convincing it to stay down. Finally, the other man won, which hurt my pride as I don't like losing. The man was bequeathed the painted prize we both wanted. The die was cast. The eagle had flown away.

A few minutes later, I was introduced as the next speaker to give the closing keynote to this group of 500 outdoor parks professionals. But even as I spoke outwardly, on the inside, I wasn't over the painting. It didn't help that the man in the audience who now owned *my* eagle had it positioned in a chair facing the stage. Thus, a 16-square-foot bald eagle glared at me from the audience, like you do.

After the speech, I engaged in the usual process of meeting incredible people, autographing books, and preparing to leave. But I noticed that people were gathering around the guy with the eagle, so I walked that way to see what was happening. Suddenly, a woman I knew from various networking spaces emerged from the crowd and said, "Mark! The guy who won the painting can't fit it into his car, so he gave it to me!"

Someone had given her the bird—and this news made me contemplate doing the same. But my better angels prevailed. "I'm so happy for you!" I said in a totally convincing way. Totally.

"Yeah!" she replied, detecting something mysterious in my voice. "Yeah."

"Yeah," I continued slyly, "Hey, so, uh . . . what would you think about me and you, well, me, I guess . . . well, what if I were to buy it from you?" I mustered a cheesy, innocent grin.

A kind smile broke out across her face. "Buy it? I don't think so, Mark." She paused for effect. "It's yours."

It was just a painting, but tears filled my eyes. It was if the eagle had stretched out its wings to embrace me (as eagles do), and now I held the painting in my hands in splendid disbelief. It was huge! Luckily, my Jeep Wrangler was big enough to do its wrangling of the painting and I sped out of there like a bank robber on the lam.

On the drive home, my plans for the eagle began flying in a different direction. When I brought it into the house, my wife's face was exactly as I had envisioned it. "Before you say anything," I interjected, "I felt a burning desire to get this eagle painting—but not for *our* wall." Her expression melted into relief.

"It's for Jobie."

Jobie is a hardworking family man and business owner—and my best friend. He'd also give you the shirt off his own back. My wife and his wife had been best friends for years, which led to us becoming best friends as well. We're so close that we named our son after him. Jobie and his wife live in Pittsburgh. They have five incredible boys who all love hockey and the Pittsburgh Penguins.

But there was about to be a new beloved bird in their life—and it ain't no penguin!

At the time, Jobie was also going through a season of extreme hardship. He had been diagnosed with stage four melanoma and his survival wasn't looking likely. A few weeks later near Christmas, life's events lined up in a way that I was able to drive to Pittsburgh to visit. I knocked on his door and to my surprise, he happened to be the only one home. He was in a hospital bed dealing with post-chemo weakness and complications. The cancer had spread throughout his whole body.

I didn't lead with the eagle painting—I didn't want to overwhelm him. He was peaceful, but obviously extremely exhausted and fatigued. After some catching up, he closed his eyes and said, "Man, I'm so glad you're here, but I have to go to sleep."

"Of course, man."

"But I just want you to know that with everything going on, I've really been working on my relationship with God."

"Really?" I asked gently. Again, you may not be a person of faith, but in Jobie's world, this was huge. He wasn't secure in his beliefs on faith either. The reality of life and death has a way of making faith a valid topic of thought and conversation.

"Yeah, I'm in the fight of my life, Mark. I don't want to leave my wife and my boys, you know?"

"I know," I said in a sad tone. It was all I could say.

"I have to trust God more. I have to trust."

Chills ran up and down my spine. *Trust* was quite the word to hear from someone lying in a bed clinging to their life. We had never talked like this, but he was desperate, so I tried to be the best friend I could by encouraging him. He just wanted peace. We said a prayer together. Afterwards, we sat in silence as tears rolled down both our faces. It's hard to explain, but that peace he was seeking was something we both felt in that moment.

Then I told him I had something for him, but I had to go downstairs to retrieve it. When I walked in the door with the beautiful monstrosity of a painting, his face lit up in a way I hadn't seen in months.

"Bro, that's the biggest and most beautiful eagle I've ever seen!"

"I know, right?" I told him the funny story of how it came into my possession. "Listen, man," I said, "in all seriousness, I feel like 'the eagle has landed' and it's a symbol that someone is watching over you." As we talked, I told him how I wanted this eagle to remind him that strength and clarity were coming for him as he continued to learn to trust.

This isn't all about faith. Trust is essential to any connection. Those who trust in others and who strive to become trustworthy for those looking for a safe place to land embody what it means to be a gift. We all face situations we can't control. Health. Job loss. Family issues. Financial stressors. When you can't see where you're going, you need someone in whom you can trust. A friend. Your faith. And in some cases, the kind word of a stranger.

This story reveals the weight trust holds in our connections on multiple levels. I had to trust the process enough to stop bidding money I didn't have. My work friend trusted me enough to give me the painting. Jobie trusted enough to open up about his trust issues. All around, trust cultivates a sense of presence and the potential for true connection.

Brené Brown uses a "marble jar" metaphor to illustrate how trust is built incrementally through small, consistent actions over time. Every time you share something with someone that's confidential, and they don't share it with others, they get a marble. When someone checks on your sick parent, they get a marble. When someone makes room for the person who has no seat in the school or company cafeteria, they get a marble.

Full marble jar friends are trusted friends. When you want to share something really private and personal, you look for these kinds of friends. Even in business, many leaders enter crises expecting their team members to trust them simply because they tell them, too. But full jar leaders don't have to ask for trust—it's already there. Everything we do (or don't do) adds or removes marbles from our trust jar.

For Jobie, he's still trusting today and is out of the woods of cancer, though his health path isn't always the smoothest. Yes, I know all stories don't have happy endings, but in all circumstances, we can still find a way to trust in the process, even when we can't predict the outcomes. Trust says that it's not all up to you. It says someone else is in the hardship with you. It reminds you that connection isn't just about interaction. It's about holding each other up in moments we can't stand on our own.

It also might help to have a gigantic eagle painting in your room reminding you to trust . . . just please ask your spouse before you bring it home.

Missed Speeches and Sensitivity—(GIFTS)

I was waiting in Dallas for my flight back to Detroit. It had been a good trip, but I was tired and hungry. I sat down in the airport restaurant and did two of my favorite things: eating and people watching.

That's when I noticed a couple eating their Panda Express together. They stuck out to me for two reasons: they looked to be in their mid-eighties and they were extremely well-dressed to be just traveling—a nice blouse and long skirt for the lady and suit and tie for the gentleman. When most people wear yoga pants in the terminal, such dapper dressers stand out.

The man was very tall, about six foot three. He walked with a cane, but he still seemed very strong, especially for his age. He also had a pin on his suit coat that stood out to me. Something within me compelled me to connect with them, so I walked across the food court to give it my best attempt.

I'm so glad I did.

I introduced myself and asked him about his pin. It was from the U.S. Marine Corps, so I thanked him for his service. Next thing I knew, Tom, Dottie, and I were sitting together and talking. I asked what brought them to the airport so dressed up. It turned out they had been there for 36 hours and counting. Their flight had been delayed over and over again because of high winds. They were supposed to be in another city in Texas to receive an award.

There was a sense of disappointment in Tom's voice. I found out they had tried three different ways to get to their destination, but all three ways had failed. Now, a backup speaker was delivering his own speech at the conference instead of Tom and Dottie. Again, I felt a nudging inside. Tom had prepared remarks to deliver that no one was going to hear, wisdom from many years of living. It shouldn't be that way.

"Tom?" I asked, "I know we're just sitting here near the Spirit Airlines gate of this terminal, but would you mind sharing your speech with me? I'd really like to hear it."

Both their faces lit up. A bolt of energy came out of Tom like lightning. "You bet, son." Passion filled his voice as he shared about what had been filling his heart for months, the need for more men to rise up and serve their families and their communities with selflessness and sacrifice. He was supposed to deliver the speech to hundreds, but instead, he delivered it to an audience of one. His tone was a time-tested mix of conviction and meekness. He wasn't harsh or judgmental. Rather, he was seasoned and gracious, breathing inspiration and grit into my younger heart. I wanted what he had and I wanted to be who he said I could be.

In the speech, he shared his story from more than 60 years earlier. As a young 19-year-old, he met Dottie after being released from the Marine brig (military jail) for drinking and fighting at the bars on base. She was the best thing that ever happened to him and now after all these decades, they were still sweethearts. They had spent much of their life together traveling the world as USMC chaplains, sharing hope with everyone they had met.

Now he was sharing it with me, and all because I had the humble honor of being sensitive to what I was feeling inside. He asked me my name and when I told him, he teared up. "Our baby's name is Mark." Of course, their youngest son would have been much older than me at the time, but Mark was still their baby.

He went on to share that he had not faced much real suffering in his life, but that two years before, he had been diagnosed with cancer. Now he was experiencing what the ancient writers described about suffering being a necessity to real living. As he sniffled, Dottie reached across the table and wiped his face with a napkin, showing him the same loving care they had shared together for over six decades. They were still smitten for each other.

When he was finished talking, I could envision how the intended audience would have risen to their feet to applaud his selfless reflections of wisdom and grace. I could see them receiving their lifetime achievement award and beaming with pride. But as I looked at them in that airport terminal, I saw them beaming just the same. Dottie leaned in and grabbed my arm, "He's been preparing these remarks for over two months and we were praying for an opportunity for him to share them. Thank you for being sensitive enough to be the answer to our prayers."

As you know, I usually fly Delta. This was the first time I had ever flown Spirit Airlines. There was a reason to it all, but I could have easily missed it among the delays, the high winds, or just the exhaustion that made me want to eat my dinner in peace and scroll on my phone to pacify my tired mind.

To share the gift of yourself in connection with others, you'll have to be sensitive to the moment and the needs of those around you. The opportunities are endless, but so are the people walking right past them with headphones in as they stare down at a screen instead of looking up at the people all around them. Sensitivity isn't a gift; it's a choice. No matter who you are, you can choose to see others and engage or respond outside of your basest feelings.

Final Reflections

In the end, the gift of connection is about becoming the gift yourself. It means being someone who leans in with grace. It means finding moments and places to exert the right kind of influence that will encourage and help the other person. Being the gift means refusing to give up the focus it takes to stay situationally present, seeing connection as something worth the trouble. It means trusting the process with courage as you invite others into the trustworthy place you are creating for them. And it means remaining sensitive to both the needs of others and the opportunities all around each of us to pursue real, genuine connection.

You are a gift. Don't ever let life's struggles or false inner messages convince you otherwise. Spend the rest of your life figuring out how to unwrap the gift of your own connection so you can share with those around you. The world will be glad you did.

Reflection

Which element of the GIFTS model feels most present in your life right now—and which one is inviting your attention and growth?

Afterword: A Letter to My Grandchildren

In the introduction, my wife encouraged me to write this book to our children's' children.

To my grandchildren,

When I was just seven years old, my Grandpa Lepine passed away. Thankfully, his memory lived on because he left little bread crumbs of his life on earth that we could follow. As a gifted musician and creator, he recorded music on an 8-track that predated the cassette tape I grew up with. Thankfully, his music and words were eventually digitized, allowing us to listen to him nearly 40 years after he was gone.

My Aunt Mary, Grandpa's daughter, preserved a few other family artifacts that made their way to me. One of these was a shadow box containing his Navy hat and the medals he earned as a World War II pilot. I eventually gave it to my cousin who served in the Army. Another heirloom was a small travel journal, about the size of a wallet, labeled *1949*. Inside were the records he kept of his business trips as a traveling salesman. In the back of this sacred little black book, he noted all of the car maintenance required during 1949. These included a muffler replacement for $10.73 and a tire rotation for $2.00. I often return to these memories as reminders of the era in which he grew up and the impact he had on my life.

I pray this book does the same for you.

You see, romanticizing the past is natural rite of passage for each generation. However, the greatest gain from our past isn't about the cost of car maintenance or where we traveled. It's the accrued value of wisdom. As you continue to navigate a tech-first world, I urge you to push back against whatever social trend tempts you to reduce your precious time making real, live memories with the ones you love the most. Technology is a great tool, but it can also be a temptation to spend our time on things that bring no return.

In the end, we don't know how much time we have. My other grandfather, Grandpa Ostach, died when he was 50 years old. I never even met him. My Grandpa Lepine died when he was 67. And I'm writing these words at 44 hoping for another 44 to go! Your time on earth is sacred and limited. Do whatever you can to push against the raging rapids of Grandpa Mark's law so you can find your footing in the ability to focus on what matter most: relationships.

If any of you are reading this and feeling lost in life, call up an old friend and meet them for a meal. If you're doubting your faith in God, great! That's the best way to grow closer to Him as work out your own beliefs. Find your way back to a church and read through the Gospel of John. Or if you are too busy to do so because you are focused on making money and finding success, take some time and read through the book of Proverbs. There are 30 chapters and you can read one a day for the month.

If you are battling screen addiction, do me a favor: try walking some trails in your local community for two weeks in a row. And leave your phone in your car when doing so. Explore music, art, sewing—just explore life outside of a screen.

Whatever stage of life you are navigating as you read these words, know that life is hard and will come with plenty of unplanned moments. These moments require friends and family to get you through them. Don't let your pride prevent you from getting help. And when all else fails, go find a place to serve someone who is in need. You'll quickly be less overwhelmed by your own situation as you pour into someone else.

And lastly, if the entire globe goes paperless and this book is no longer able to be placed on a bookshelf in your house or local library (if they still exist), I pray that your presence alone will embody the essence of these pages.

Love always,
Grandpa Ostach

Appendix: Generative Dialogue Questions

These questions can help you avoid shallow conversations, gain new insights, and strengthen connections.

Opening the Door (Warm-Up)

These gently pull people out of autopilot:

- What has been giving you energy lately?
- What's something simple that made you smile this week?
- What's one thing you're grateful for right now?

Attention and Presence

These invite reflection about how people are actually living:

- What tends to pull you away from the present moment?
- What's something you wish you had more time for?
- When do you feel most at peace?

Identity and Becoming

These open deeper self-awareness:

- How would someone who knows you well describe you?
- What part of yourself have you grown into over the past few years?
- What are you still learning about yourself?

Dreams and Desire

These reveal what's alive inside someone:

- What's something you're quietly hoping for?
- If fear wasn't in the way, what would you go after?
- What feels like the next chapter of your life?

Resilience and Meaning

These invite story and depth:

- What's a challenge that changed you?
- What's something you've survived that you're proud of?
- Who helped you through a hard season?

Connection and Relationships

These build emotional safety:

- Who makes you feel most like yourself?
- What's something someone did for you that you'll never forget?
- What do you value most in friendships?

Notes

Introduction

1. Europol Innovation Lab, *Facing Reality? Law Enforcement and the Challenge of Deepfakes* (The Hague: Europol, 2022), https://www.europol.europa.eu/cms/sites/default/files/documents/Europol_Innovation_Lab_Facing_Reality_Law_Enforcement_And_The_Challenge_Of_Deepfakes.pdf.

Chapter 1

1. Josh Howarth, "Alarming Average Screen Time Statistics (2024)," Exploding Topics, June 24, 2024, https://explodingtopics.com/blog/screen-time-stats.

Chapter 2

1. Tamim Mobayed, "Is Social Media the New Smoking?" *Psychology Today*, November 14, 2024.
2. Jonathan Haidt, *The Anxious Generation: How the Great Rewiring of Childhood Is Causing an Epidemic of Mental Illness* (New York: Penguin Press, 2024).
3. Office of the Surgeon General, *Our Epidemic of Loneliness and Isolation: The U.S. Surgeon General's Advisory on the Healing Effects of Social Connection and Community* (Washington, DC: U.S. Department

of Health and Human Services, 2023), https://www.hhs.gov/sites/default/files/surgeon-general-social-connection-advisory.pdf.

4. WHO Commission on Social Connection, *From Loneliness to Social Connection: Charting a Path to Healthier Societies* (Geneva: World Health Organization, 2025), https://www.who.int/publications/i/item/978240112360.
5. World Health Organization, "Social Connection Linked to Improved Health and Reduced Risk of Early Death," news release, June 30, 2025, https://www.who.int/news/item/30-06-2025-social-connection-linked-to-improved-heath-and-reduced-risk-of-early-death.
6. Dylan Butts, "Australia Is Trying to Enforce the First Teen Social Media Ban. Governments Worldwide Are Watching," CNBC, December 10, 2025, https://www.cnbc.com/2025/12/10/australia-16-year-old-teens-ban-social-media-policy-law-ig-tiktok-fb-reddit-youtube-snapchat.html.
7. Bobby Allyn. "Jury Finds Meta and Google Negligent in Social Media Harms Trial," All Things Considered, March 25, 2026, https://www.npr.org/2026/03/25/nx-s1-5746125/meta-youtube-social-media-trial-verdict.

Chapter 3

1. Amy is the founder of the Digital Wellness Institute and someone I collaborated with out on the speaking and writing circuit. Since 2020, the Digital Wellness Institute has led the global movement to measure how technology affects human thriving. I helped to develop the Digital Flourishing® Survey, the world's first scientifically validated survey for digital well-being. Today, more than 40,000 individuals across 62 countries have taken the survey—helping organizations, schools, and communities translate data into meaningful action. See https://www.digitalwellnessinstitute.com and https://amyblankson.com.

Chapter 4

1. "You'll Probably Spend at Least 17 Years of Your Adult Life Online," *Fortune Well*, September 25, 2024, https://fortune.com/well/article/screen-time-over-lifespan.

Chapter 5

1. Boris Artzybasheff, "The Computer in Society, Cover Illustration," *TIME*, April 2, 1965, https://content.time.com/time.covers/0,16641,19650402,00.html.
2. "The Cybernated Generation," *TIME*, April 2, 1965, 84–92.
3. Ibid.
4. Roman Family Center, University of Chicago Booth School of Business, "Think Better with Adam Alter," accessed November 10, 2025, https://www.chicagobooth.edu/research/roman/stories/think-better-with-adam-alter.
5. Cal Newport, *A World Without Email: Reimagining Work in an Age of Communication Overload* (New York: Portfolio/Penguin, 2021).
6. Brian Tracy, *Get Smart!: How to Think and Act Like the Most Successful and Highest-Paid People in Every Field* (New York: TarcherPerigee, 2016), 31.
7. Boston University, "Will Sharks Scare, or Attract, Cape Cod Tourists?" BU Today, July 23, 2019, https://www.bu.edu/articles/2019/cape-cod-tourism-sharks.
8. Ibid.
9. Christopher Muther, "Avoid the Conventional for 2019," *Boston Globe*, January 6, 2019, https://apps.bostonglobe.com/lifestyle/travel/2019/01/06/muther-travel-2019-suggestions/.
10. Frank Langfitt, "Covering the Sago Mine Disaster," Nieman Reports (Summer 2006), https://niemanreports.org/covering-the-sago-mine-disaster/.
11. Kensington Church, Troy MI, Sermon from Spring of 2012.
12. Silicon Valley insider on why smartphones are "slot machines," https://www.youtube.com/watch?v=gvQxtotEX-M.
13. https://www.walkforwardjournal.com/

Chapter 6

1. Scott Galloway, "Scott Galloway Talks 'Notes on Being a Man,' Modern Masculinity," *TODAY*, November 3, 2025, YouTube video, https://www.youtube.com/watch?v=1QFlCslEnGg.
2. Jonathan Haidt, *The Anxious Generation: How the Great Rewiring of Childhood Is Causing an Epidemic of Mental Illness* (New York:Penguin Press, 2024).
3. Ginny Yurich, *Until the Streetlights Come On: How a Return to Play Brightens Our Present and Prepares Kids for an Uncertain Future* (Grand Rapids, MI: Baker Books, 2023), back cover.
4. Julie Lythcott-Haims, "How to Raise Successful Kids—Without Over-Parenting," TED Talk, November 2016, https://www.ted.com/talks/julie_lythcott_haims_how_to_raise_successful_kids_without_over_parenting; or her book How to Raise an Adult (New York: Henry Holt, 2015).
5. Mark E. Bardgett, Melissa Depenbrock, Nathan Downs, Megan Points, and Leonard Green, "Dopamine Modulates Effort-Based Decision-Making in Rats," *Behavioral Neuroscience* 123, no. 6 (2009): 1194–1204,https://pmc.ncbi.nlm.nih.gov/articles/PMC2791340/.
6. Ibid.
7. Henry Kissinger, "Man of the Year: They Are Fated to Succeed," *TIME*,January2,1978,https://time.com/archive/6849611/man-of-the-year-they-are-fated-to-succeed/.
8. Søren Kierkegaard, *The Concept of Anxiety: A Simple Psychologically Orienting Deliberation on the Dogmatic Issue of Hereditary Sin*, trans. Reidar Thomte (Princeton, NJ: Princeton University Press, 1980), 61.
9. Jon Acuff, *Soundtracks: The Surprising Solution to Overthinking* (New York: WaterBrook, 2022), 97–98.
10. A classic book I often recommend to everyone I meet in these situations is *Purpose-Driven Life* by Rick Warren.

Chapter 7

1. Britt Frank, *The Science of Stuck: Breaking Through Inertia to Find Your Path Forward* (New York: TarcherPerigee, 2022).
2. Richard C. Schwartz, *Introduction to Internal Family Systems* (New York: St. Martin's Essentials, 2023).
3. Britt Frank, *Align Your Mind: Tame Your Inner Critic and Make Peace with Your Shadow Using the Power of Parts Work* (New York: Tarcher, 2025).
4. Parker J. Palmer, *Let Your Life Speak: Listening for the Voice of Vocation* (San Francisco: Jossey-Bass, 2024).
5. Parker J. Palmer, *Let Your Life Speak: Listening for the Voice of Vocation* (San Francisco: Jossey-Bass, 1999), 16.
6. Ibid., 5.
7. Richard Langworth, "Q&A: 'Black Dog'—Churchill and Depression," The Churchill Project, Hillsdale College, accessed December 1, 2025, https://winstonchurchill.hillsdale.edu/churchill-and-depression.
8. Dallas Willard and Gary Black Jr., The Divine Conspiracy Continued: Fulfilling God's Kingdom on Earth (New York: HarperOne), 117.
9. Bob Goff, *Love Does: Discover a Secretly Incredible Life in an Ordinary World* (Nashville: Thomas Nelson, 2012).

Chapter 8

1. Seattle Chamber of Connection, "6 Points of Connection," accessed December 3, 2025, https://www.seattlechamberofconnection.org/6pointsofconnection.
2. Gary Chapman, *The Five Love Languages: How to Express Heartfelt Commitment to Your Mate* (Chicago: Northfield Publishing, 1992).
3. Joseph Luft, *Group Processes: An Introduction to Group Dynamics* (Palo Alto, CA: National Press Books, 1963).

4. Seattle Chamber of Connection, "6 Points of Connection," accessed December 3, 2025, https://www.seattlechamberofconnection.org/6pointsofconnection.
5. Robert B. Cialdini, *Influence: The Psychology of Persuasion*, rev. ed. (New York: Harper Business, 2006).
6. Ray Oldenburg, *The Great Good Place: Cafés, Coffee Shops, Bookstores, Bars, Hair Salons, and Other Hangouts at the Heart of a Community* (New York: Paragon House, 1989).
7. William Isaacs, *Dialogue and the Art of Thinking Together: A Pioneering Approach to Communicating in Business and in Life* (New York: Currency/Doubleday, 1999), 242–290.

Chapter 9

1. Brené Brown, "The Power of Vulnerability," filmed June 2010 at TEDxHouston, Houston, TX, video, 20:19, https://www.ted.com/talks/brene_brown_the_power_of_vulnerability.
2. Brené Brown, *The Gifts of Imperfection: Let Go of Who You Think You're Supposed to Be and Embrace Who You Are* (Center City, MN: Hazelden Publishing, 2010), 20.
3. Brené Brown, *I Thought It Was Just Me (but It Isn't): Making the Journey from "What Will People Think?" to "I Am Enough"* (New York: Penguin, 2007), 16.
4. "The Enneagram: A Primer for Psychiatry Residents," https://psychiatryonline.org/doi/10.1176/appi.ajp-rj.2020.150301.
5. Imperva, "2025 Bad Bot Report: The Rise of Automated Traffic," Imperva Research Labs, 2025.
6. Samuel C. Woolley and Philip N. Howard, *Computational Propaganda: Political Parties, Politicians, and Political Manipulation on Social Media, Oxford Studies in Digital Politics* (Oxford Internet Institute, University of Oxford, 2018).
7. Carnegie Mellon University, Software and Societal Systems Department, research on bot prevalence and online participation patterns.

8. Stanford Internet Observatory, "Measuring Inauthentic Behavior and AI-Enabled Influence Operations," Stanford Cyber Policy Center.
9. Maria Carolina Juvêncio Francisquini, Thais Maria de Souza Silva, Géssika Castilho dos Santos, Rodrigo de Oliveira Barbosa, Pedro Henrique Garcia Dias, Ariel Bello Ruiz, Jadson Marcio da Silva, and Neto A. Stabelini, "Associations of Screen Time with Symptoms of Stress, Anxiety, and Depression in Adolescents," *The Revista Paulista de Pediatria* 43 (2024): e2023250. doi: 10.1590/1984-0462/2025/43/2023250.

Chapter 10

1. Albert Bandura, *Social Learning Theory* (New York: Prentice Hall, 1977).
2. Gustave Le Bon, *The Crowd: A Study of the Popular Mind* (Paris: Librairie Felxi Alcan, 1895).
3. Ragnar Purje, "The Impact of Tech on Young Minds," *Psychology Today*, March 3, 2026. https://www.psychologytoday.com/us/blog/recovery-from-brain-injury/202602/the-impact-of-tech-on-young-minds; Organization for Economic Co-operation and Development (OECD), *Students, Computers and Learning: Making the Connection* (Paris: PISA, OECD Publishing, 2015).
4. American Psychological Association, *Reward Systems and Behavioral Reinforcement* (Washington, DC: Author, n.d.).
5. Michael B. Robb and Supreet Mann, *Betting on Boys: Understanding Gambling Among Adolescent Boys* (San Francisco: Common Sense Media, 2026). https://www.commonsensemedia.org/sites/default/files/research/report/2026-betting-on-boys-report_final-for-web.pdf
6. American Psychological Association, *Reward Systems and Behavioral Reinforcement.*

7. Nicholas Carr, *The Shallows: What the Internet Is Doing to Our Brains* (New York: W. W. Norton & Company, 2010); Jonathan Haidt, *The Anxious Generation: How the Great Rewiring of Childhood Is Causing an Epidemic of Mental Illness* (New York: Penguin Press, 2024).
8. Vittorio Gallese, Luciano Fadiga, Leonardo Fogassi, and Giacomo Rizzolatti, "Action Recognition in the Premotor Cortex," Brain 119, no. 2 (April 1996): 593–609.
9. Ronald Reagan, Commencement Address, Eureka College, May 9, 1982.

Chapter 11

1. Tommy Spaulding, *The Gift of Influence: Creating Life-Changing and Lasting Impact in Your Everyday Interactions* (New York: Convergent Books, 2022), 1–3.
2. John C. Maxwell, *The 21 Irrefutable Laws of Leadership: Follow Them and People Will Follow You*, rev. ed. (Nashville: Thomas Nelson, 2007), 13.
3. Daniel J. Siegel and Tina Payne Bryson, *The Whole-Brain Child: 12 Revolutionary Strategies to Nurture Your Child's Developing Mind* (New York: Delacorte Press, 2011), 38–42.
4. Becky A. Bailey, *Conscious Discipline: Building Resilient Classrooms*, expanded and updated ed. (Oviedo, FL: Loving Guidance, 2015); "Safe Place Breathing Icons," Conscious Discipline, accessed December 15, 2025, https://consciousdiscipline.com/resources/breathing-star/.
5. Bailey, Conscious Discipline; "Breathing/Composure Exercises," Conscious Discipline, accessed December 15, 2025, https://sites.google.com/apps.pusd.org/consciousdiscipline/resources-structures/breathingcomposure-exercises.
6. "Pretzel Breathing Technique for Children," *Healthy Minds Therapy* (blog), April 30, 2021, https://healthymindstherapy.blog/2021/04/30/pretzel-breathing-technique-for-children/; "Safe Place Breathing Icons," Conscious Discipline.

7. "Drain," Conscious Discipline, January 24, 2019, https://consciousdiscipline.com/memberships/free-resources/shuberts-home/laundry-room/drain/; "Faucet Breathing: Kind Karma Kids Breathing Technique for Draining Out Stress and Anxiousness," Kind Karma Worldwide, June 3, 2024, https://www.kindkarmaworldwide.org/post/faucet-breathing-kind-karma-kids-breathing-technique-for-draining-out-stress-and-anxiousness.

Acknowledgments

The writing process requires feedback, support, and encouragement. I am grateful to the many people who contributed to this work and made it possible.

First and foremost, John Driver, I had hoped to collaborate with you for more than five years, and when that opportunity finally arrived through this book, it brought a deep sense of fulfillment. Your ability to shape the stories and research while preserving the tone, truth, and timing of my words was invaluable. You also helped introduce humor, which was an important goal for this project. Trusting another voice in the shaping of my work required a level of openness that did not come easily, and I am grateful for your guidance throughout the writing and revision process. Your insight, patience, and friendship were true gifts.

To my wife, Ksenija. Our story is woven throughout these pages. Sharing personal moments of our life together, especially in such a public way requires vulnerability. My hope is that our experiences encourage others as they navigate marriage, family, and the tension of living in a modern world filled with constant distraction. The digital challenges we face as a family are deeply relatable, and I am grateful for your trust in allowing our story to be shared as a point of connection rather than critique. I love you lovies.

To my children. Thank you for the countless early-morning visits to my basement office offering hugs in your pajamas while you were just waking up and I was already deep into edits and coffee. I hope this book is something you will one day share with your own children as a reminder of the connection we shared as a family during this season of life.

To my parents. Thank you for the countless lessons you've taught me and the love you've always given me. I love you both dearly.

To my prayer partners and encouragers.

Michael Hahn, your early-morning check-ins and shared sense of calling were a consistent source of encouragement. You are truly my brother from another mother!

Michael Fencil, you have been with me since the first page of my first book. Your steady presence, generosity with time, and ability to ground me in the truth during moments of discouragement have been invaluable.

Stephanie Jones, you are a true prayer warrior. Your snail mail, texts, and literal mustard seeds reminded me to stay the course. Thank you for your obedience to the whisper and overall friendship.

Jeremiah Roberts, your voicemails are ones I return to often. Thank you for reminding me that inspired writing flows from God's Spirit working within us. Your faith and encouragement have touched many.

James Kosty, we've known each other since sixth grade. You have the most natural talent I've ever seen in someone. Thanks for checking in with me to make sure I was staying on path with this book. You are a lifelong friend and I love you.

Chad Brent, your editing, reviewing, suggesting, and phone calls to and from the office were momentum builders behind this book. You are one of my best friends. I look forward to our next round of karaoke soon.

To the OakDads. In a season where fatherhood demands full presence, I am grateful for your fellowship, prayer, and friendship—from parking-lot conversations to late-night bonfires at Devin's to countless coffee conversations. Your friendship helped guard against isolation and reminded me of the power of community with men doing life together.

To my editorial team at Wiley. Thank you for recognizing my passion at the intersection of psychology, technology, and business, and for providing the opportunity to share this work on a broader platform.

To Shawn McConnel, you are the most talented creative I know. Thanks for bringing this book cover to life. I can't wait to meet up for coffee and some sunshine to celebrate another year of friendship.

To you, the reader. Thank you for investing your time and attention in this book. I hope you found encouragement, insight, and inspiration along the way.

To the many individuals whose stories appear throughout these pages: my friends, family members, and strangers encountered along my travels, thank you for the moments of connection that shaped this work.

Finally, I give thanks to Jesus for sustaining the vision for the book, provision to write it, and grace throughout this process.

About the Author

Mark Ostach helps people find the courage to connect. A globally recognized speaker on human connection and digital wellness and frequently featured in the *USA Today*, Mark has done two TED Talks, written three books, and spoken to thousands of people encouraging them to embrace a spirit of courage through vulnerability.

Mark has degrees in psychology, technology, and an interest in behavioral neuroscience. His mission is to remind the world that human connection is the most powerful connection we have. When he's not on the road, he enjoys spending time outside with his wife, their two children, and three dogs. To book Mark to speak at your conference or event, please visit https://markostach.com/.

Index